enVision® Florida MATHEMATICS

Volume 2 Topics 9-15

Authors

Randall I. Charles
Professor Emeritus
Department of Mathematics
San Jose State University
San Jose, California

Jennifer Bay-Williams
Professor of Mathematics Education
College of Education and Human
Development
University of Louisville
Louisville, Kentucky

Robert Q. Berry, III
Professor of Mathematics Education
Department of Curriculum,
Instruction and Special Education
University of Virginia
Charlottesville, Virginia

Janet H. Caldwell
Professor Emerita
Department of Mathematics
Rowan University
Glassboro, New Jersey

Zachary Champagne
Assistant in Research
Florida Center for Research in Science,
Technology, Engineering, and
Mathematics (FCR-STEM)
Jacksonville, Florida

Juanita Copley
Professor Emerita, College of Education
University of Houston
Houston, Texas

Warren Crown
Professor Emeritus of Mathematics
Education
Graduate School of Education
Rutgers University
New Brunswick, New Jersey

Francis (Skip) Fennell
Professor Emeritus of
Education and Graduate and
Professional Studies
McDaniel College
Westminster, Maryland

Karen Karp
Visiting Professor of
Mathematics Education
School of Education
Johns Hopkins University
Baltimore, Maryland

Stuart J. Murphy
Visual Learning Specialist
Boston, Massachusetts

Jane F. Schielack
Professor Emerita
Department of Mathematics
Texas A&M University
College Station, Texas

Jennifer M. Suh
Associate Professor for
Mathematics Education
George Mason University
Fairfax, Virginia

Jonathan A. Wray
Mathematics Supervisor
Howard County Public Schools
Ellicott City, Maryland

 Pearson

Glenview, Illinois   Boston, Massachusetts
Chandler, Arizona   New York, New York

Mathematicians

Roger Howe
Professor of Mathematics
Yale University
New Haven, Connecticut

Gary Lippman
Professor of Mathematics and
Computer Science
California State University, East Bay
Hayward, California

ELL Consultants

Janice R. Corona
Independent Education Consultant
Dallas, Texas

Jim Cummins
Professor
The University of Toronto
Toronto, Canada

Florida Reviewers

Robert Curran
Instructional Math Coach
Duval County Public Schools
Jacksonville, Florida

Megan Hanes
Math Coach
Marion County Public Schools
Ocala, Florida

Connie Jeppessen
Elementary Math
Instructional Coach
Hernando County School District
Brooksville, Florida

Jacqueline LeJeune
Mathematics Academic Coach
Hillsborough County
Public Schools
Tampa, Florida

Lesley Lynn
Academic Math Coach
Hillsborough County
Public Schools
Tampa, Florida

**Christina Pescatrice
Mrozek**
Assistant Principal
Orange County Public Schools
Orlando, Florida

Pam Root
Teacher
Felix A. Williams Elementary
Martin County School District
Stuart, Florida

Ashley Russell
Elementary Math Teacher
Chets Creek Elementary
Jacksonville, Florida

Tiffany Thibault
Lead Teacher
Lake County Schools
Tavares, Florida

Shanna Uhe
Math Academic Coach
Hillsborough County
Public Schools
Tampa, Florida

ISBN-13: 978-0-13-491075-8
ISBN-10: 0-13-491075-3

5 19

You'll be using these digital resources throughout the year!

Digital Resources

Go to PearsonRealize.com

 Interactive Student Edition
Access online or offline.

 Visual Learning
Interact with visual learning animations.

 Activity
Solve a problem and share your thinking.

 Interactive Additional Practice Workbook
Access online or offline.

 Videos
Watch Math Practices Animations, Another Look Videos, and clips to support 3-Act Math.

 Practice Buddy
Do interactice practice online.

 Math Tools
Explore math with digital tools.

 Games
Play math games to help you learn.

 A-Z Glossary
Read and listen in English and Spanish.

 Assessment
Show what you've learned.

PEARSON realize. Everything you need for math anytime, anywhere

F3

Contents

Digital Resources at PearsonRealize.com

TOPICS

And remember your Interactive Student Edition is available at PearsonRealize.com!

PearsonRealize.com

This shows how you can make 259 using place-value blocks.

TOPIC 9
Numbers to 1,000

Contents

This shows how you can use mental math and place-value blocks to find 243 + 100.

243 + 100 = ?

Add 1 hundred

TOPIC 10
Add Within 1,000 Using Models and Strategies

PearsonRealize.com

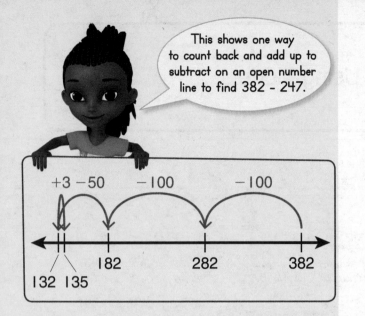

This shows one way to count back and add up to subtract on an open number line to find 382 – 247.

+3 −50   −100   −100

132 135   182   282   382

TOPIC 11
Subtract Within 1,000 Using Models and Strategies

Contents

This shows how to measure to the nearest inch. The eraser is about 2 inches long.

INCHES
0   1   2

halfway mark

TOPIC 12
Measuring Length

This shows a way you can draw a cube.

TOPIC 13
Shapes and Their Attributes

Contents

This shows how you can represent whole numbers as lengths and subtract on a number line.

Amelia buys 17 feet of rope. She cuts off 8 feet of rope to make a jump rope.

How many feet of rope does she have left?

TOPIC 14
More Addition, Subtraction, and Length

This picture graph shows data and can be used to solve problems.

Favorite Ball Games	
Baseball	𝑥 𝑥
Soccer	𝑥 𝑥 𝑥 𝑥 𝑥 𝑥 𝑥 𝑥
Tennis	𝑥 𝑥 𝑥 𝑥

Each 𝑥 = 1 student

TOPIC 15
Graphs and Data

Contents

Dear Families,

The standards on the following pages describe the math that students will learn this year.

MATHEMATICS FLORIDA STANDARDS (MAFS)

DOMAIN: Operations and Algebraic Thinking

MAFS.2.OA.1 Represent and solve problems involving addition and subtraction.

MAFS.2.OA.1.1 Use addition and subtraction within 100 to solve one- and two-step word problems involving situations of adding to, taking from, putting together, taking apart, and comparing, with unknowns in all positions, e.g., by using drawings and equations with a symbol for the unknown number to represent the problem.

MAFS.2.OA.1.a Determine the unknown whole number in an equation relating four or more whole numbers. *For example, determine the unknown number that makes the equation true in the equations*

$37 + 10 + 10 = \_\_\_\_\_ + 18$, $? - 6 = 13 - 4$, and $15 - 9 = 6 + \square$.

MAFS.2.OA.2 Add and subtract within 20.

MAFS.2.OA.2.2 Fluently add and subtract within 20 using mental strategies. By end of Grade 2, know from memory all sums of two one-digit numbers.

MAFS.2.OA.3 Work with equal groups of objects to gain foundations for multiplication.

MAFS.2.OA.3.3 Determine whether a group of objects (up to 20) has an odd or even number of members, e.g., by pairing objects or counting them by 2s; write an equation to express an even number as a sum of two equal addends.

MAFS.2.OA.3.4 Use addition to find the total number of objects arranged in rectangular arrays with up to 5 rows and up to 5 columns; write an equation to express the total as a sum of equal addends.

🟠 Florida Grade 2 Standards

DOMAIN: Number and Operations in Base Ten

MAFS.2.NBT.1 Understand place value.

MAFS.2.NBT.1.1 Understand that the three digits of a three-digit number represent amounts of hundreds, tens, and ones; e.g., 706 equals 7 hundreds, 0 tens, and 6 ones. Understand the following as special cases:

MAFS.2.NBT.1.1.a 100 can be thought of as a bundle of ten tens—called a "hundred."

MAFS.2.NBT.1.1.b The numbers 100, 200, 300, 400, 500, 600, 700, 800, 900 refer to one, two, three, four, five, six, seven, eight, or nine hundreds (and 0 tens and 0 ones).

MAFS.2.NBT.1.2 Count within 1000; skip-count by 5s, 10s, and 100s.

MAFS.2.NBT.1.3 Read and write numbers to 1000 using base-ten numerals, number names, and expanded form.

MAFS.2.NBT.1.4 Compare two three-digit numbers based on meanings of the hundreds, tens, and ones digits, using >, =, and < symbols to record the results of comparisons.

MAFS.2.NBT.2 Use place value understanding and properties of operations to add and subtract.

MAFS.2.NBT.2.5 Fluently add and subtract within 100 using strategies based on place value, properties of operations, and/or the relationship between addition and subtraction.

MAFS.2.NBT.2.6 Add up to four two-digit numbers using strategies based on place value and properties of operations.

MAFS.2.NBT.2.7 Add and subtract within 1000, using concrete models or drawings and strategies based on place value, properties of operations, and/or the relationship between addition and subtraction; relate the strategy to a written method. Understand that in adding or subtracting three-digit numbers, one adds or subtracts hundreds and hundreds, tens and tens, ones and ones; and sometimes it is necessary to compose or decompose tens or hundreds.

MAFS.2.NBT.2.8 Mentally add 10 or 100 to a given number 100–900, and mentally subtract 10 or 100 from a given number 100–900.

MAFS.2.NBT.2.9 Explain why addition and subtraction strategies work, using place value and the properties of operations.

Florida Grade 2 Standards

DOMAIN: Measurement and Data

MAFS.2.MD.1 Measure and estimate lengths in standard units.

MAFS.2.MD.1.1 Measure the length of an object to the nearest inch, foot, centimeter, or meter by selecting and using appropriate tools such as rulers, yardsticks, meter sticks, and measuring tapes.

MAFS.2.MD.1.2 Describe the inverse relationship between the size of a unit and number of units needed to measure a given object. *Example: Suppose the perimeter of a room is lined with one-foot rulers. Now, suppose we want to line it with yardsticks instead of rulers. Will we need more or fewer yardsticks than rulers to do the job? Explain your answer.*

MAFS.2.MD.1.3 Estimate lengths using units of inches, feet, yards, centimeters, and meters.

MAFS.2.MD.1.4 Measure to determine how much longer one object is than another, expressing the length difference in terms of a standard length unit.

MAFS.2.MD.2 Relate addition and subtraction to length.

MAFS.2.MD.2.5 Use addition and subtraction within 100 to solve word problems involving lengths that are given in the same units, e.g., by using drawings (such as drawings of rulers) and equations with a symbol for the unknown number to represent the problem.

MAFS.2.MD.2.6 Represent whole numbers as lengths from 0 on a number line diagram with equally spaced points corresponding to the numbers 0, 1, 2, ..., and represent whole-number sums and differences within 100 on a number line diagram.

MAFS.2.MD.3 Work with time and money.

MAFS.2.MD.3.7 Tell and write time from analog and digital clocks to the nearest five minutes.

MAFS.2.MD.3.8 Solve one- and two-step word problems involving dollar bills (singles, fives, tens, twenties, and hundreds) or coins (quarters, dimes, nickels, and pennies) using $ and ¢ symbols appropriately. Word problems may involve addition, subtraction, and equal groups situations. *Example: The cash register shows that the total for your purchase is 59¢. You gave the cashier three quarters. How much change should you receive from the cashier?*

MAFS.2.MD.3.8.a Identify the value of coins and paper currency.

MAFS.2.MD.3.8.b Compute the value of any combination of coins within one dollar.

MAFS.2.MD.3.8.c Compute the value of any combinations of dollars (e.g., If you have three ten-dollar bills, one five-dollar bill, and two one-dollar bills, how much money do you have?).

MAFS.2.MD.3.8.d Relate the value of pennies, nickels, dimes, and quarters to other coins and to the dollar (e.g., There are five nickels in one quarter. There are two nickels in one dime. There are two and a half dimes in one quarter. There are twenty nickels in one dollar).

MAFS.2.MD.4 Represent and interpret data.

MAFS.2.MD.4.9 Generate measurement data by measuring lengths of several objects to the nearest whole unit, or by making repeated measurements of the same object. Show the measurements by making a line plot, where the horizontal scale is marked off in whole-number units.

MAFS.2.MD.4.10 Draw a picture graph and a bar graph (with single-unit scale) to represent a data set with up to four categories. Solve simple put-together, take-apart, and compare problems using information presented in a bar graph.

Florida Grade 2 Standards

DOMAIN: Geometry

MAFS.2.G.1 Reason with shapes and their attributes.

MAFS.2.G.1.1 Recognize and draw shapes having specified attributes, such as a given number of angles or a given number of equal faces. Identify triangles, quadrilaterals, pentagons, hexagons, and cubes.

MAFS.2.G.1.2 Partition a rectangle into rows and columns of same-size squares and count to find the total number of them.

MAFS.2.G.1.3 Partition circles and rectangles into two, three, or four equal shares, describe the shares using the words *halves*, *thirds*, *half of*, *a third of*, etc., and describe the whole as two halves, three thirds, four fourths. Recognize that equal shares of identical wholes need not have the same shape.

MATHEMATICAL PRACTICES

MAFS.K12.MP.1.1 Make sense of problems and persevere in solving them.

MAFS.K12.MP.2.1 Reason abstractly and quantitatively.

MAFS.K12.MP.3.1 Construct viable arguments and critique the reasoning of others.

MAFS.K12.MP.4.1 Model with mathematics.

MAFS.K12.MP.5.1 Use appropriate tools strategically.

MAFS.K12.MP.6.1 Attend to precision.

MAFS.K12.MP.7.1 Look for and make use of structure.

MAFS.K12.MP.8.1 Look for and express regularity in repeated reasoning.

LANGUAGE ARTS FLORIDA STANDARDS (LAFS)

LAFS.2.SL.1 Comprehension and Collaboration

LAFS.2.SL.1.1 Participate in collaborative conversations with diverse partners about grade 2 topics and texts with peers and adults in small and larger groups.

    a. Follow agreed-upon rules for discussions (e.g., gaining the floor in respectful ways, listening to others with care, speaking one at a time about the topics and texts under discussion).

    b. Build on others' talk in conversations by linking their comments to the remarks of others.

    c. Ask for clarification and further explanation as needed about the topics and texts under discussion

LAFS.2.SL.1.2 Recount or describe key ideas or details from a text read aloud or information presented orally or through other media.

LAFS.2.SL.1.3 Ask and answer questions about what a speaker says in order to clarify comprehension, gather additional information, or deepen understanding of a topic or issue.

LAFS.2.W.1 Text Types and Purposes

LAFS.2.W.1.2 Write informative/explanatory texts in which they introduce a topic, use facts and definitions to develop points, and provide a concluding statement or section.

ENGLISH LANGUAGE DEVELOPMENT STANDARDS (ELDS)

ELD.K12.ELL.MA Language of Mathematics

ELD.K12.ELL.MA.1 English language learners communicate information, ideas and concepts necessary for academic success in the content area of Mathematics.

ELD.K12.ELL.SI Language of Social and Instructional Purposes

ELD.K12.ELL.SI.1 English language learners communicate for social and instructional purposes within the school setting.

Math Practices and Problem Solving Handbook

The **Math Practices and Problem Solving Handbook** is available at PearsonRealize.com.

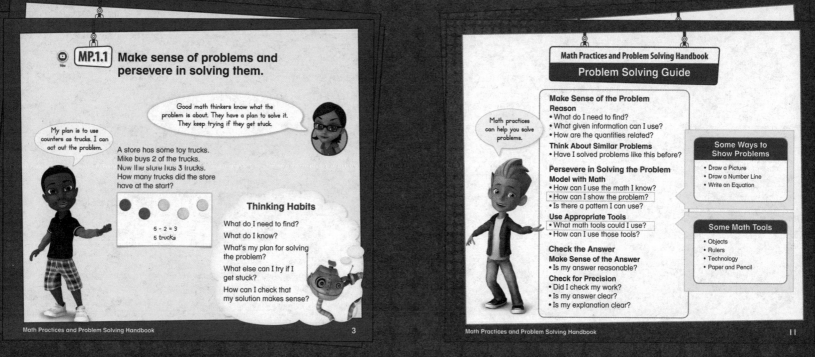

Math Practices

Problem Solving Guide
Problem Solving Recording Sheet

Numbers to 1,000

Essential Question: How can you count, read, and show numbers to 1,000?

Digital Resources

Interactive Student Edition · Activity · Visual Learning · Video · Practice

Assessment · Games · Tools · Glossary

Look at the model of a bird! How many pieces do you think it took to make it?

What else could you make with the same pieces?

Wow! Let's do this project and learn more.

MAFS.2.NBT.1.1, 2.NBT.1.1.a, 2.NBT.1.1.b, 2.NBT.1.2, 2.NBT.1.3, 2.NBT.1.4, 2.NBT.2.8
MAFS.K12. MP.1.1, MP.2.1, MP.3.1, MP.4.1, MP.5.1, MP.6.1, MP.7.1, MP.8.1

enVision STEM Project: Breaking Apart and Putting Together

Find Out Collect sets of building blocks. Take turns and work together. Use the blocks to build a model. Then take that model apart and use the same blocks to build a different model.

Journal: Make a Book Show your models in a book. In your book, also:

• Tell how many pieces you used to build your models.

• Show how to use place-value blocks to model different names for the same number.

Name _____

Review What You Know

1. Circle the coin with the **least value**. Put a square around the coin with the **greatest value**.

2. Circle the number that has 5 **ones** and 4 **tens**.

54

45

40

5

3. Tom is having breakfast. The minute hand on the clock shows **half past 7 o'clock**. Circle the time on the clock.

7:15 a.m.

7:30 a.m.

7:15 p.m.

7:30 p.m.

Counting Money

4. Circle coins that total 37¢.

Breaking Apart Numbers

5. Break apart each number into tens and ones.

23 = _____ + _____

47 = _____ + _____

96 = _____ + _____

Math Story

6. Howie has $13. A backpack costs $30. How much more money does Howie need to buy the backpack?

$_____

Name _____

PROJECT 9A

Which are the hottest planets in our solar system?

Project: Make a Planets Poster

PROJECT 9B

What is the height of the tallest waterfall in the world?

Project: Design a Waterfall Guide

PROJECT 9C

How much do large animals weigh?

Project: Create an Animal Riddle Booklet

Makes Cents

▶ Video

Before watching the video, think:

How can you save money you earn or find? What are some good places to put your money? What are some good ways to sort your money?

MAFS.K12.MP.4.1 Model with mathematics. **Also MP.1.1, MP.6.1**
MAFS.2.NBT.1.2 Count within 1000; skip-count by 5s, 10s, and 100s.
Also 2.NBT.1.1, 2.NBT.1.3, 2.NBT.2.8, 2.MD.3.8

© Pearson Education, Inc. 2

Solve & Share

What is another way to show 100? Draw a picture and explain.

I can ...
understand place value and count by hundreds to 1,000.

MAFS.2.NBT.1.1.a Understand that 100 can be thought of as a bundle of ten tens — called a "hundred." Also 2.NBT.1.1.b MAFS.K12.MP.5.1, MP.7.1

Way 1

Way 2

10 ones make 1 ten.

10 tens make 1 hundred.

10 hundreds make 1 **thousand**.

What is the number?

You can count by hundreds to 1,000!

900 equals 9 hundreds, 0 tens, and 0 ones.

Convince Me! 10 ones make 1 ten. 10 tens make 1 hundred. 10 hundreds make 1 thousand. Do you see a pattern? Explain.

☆ **Guided Practice** ☆ Complete each sentence. Use place-value blocks and your workmat to help.

1.

__600__ equals __6__ hundreds, __0__ tens, and __0__ ones.

2.

_____ equals _____ hundreds, _____ tens, and _____ ones.

Topic 9 | Lesson 1

Name _____

☆ Independent Practice ☆   Complete each sentence. Use models if needed.

3.

_____ equals _____ hundreds, _____ tens, and _____ ones.

4.

_____ equals _____ hundreds, _____ tens, and _____ ones.

5.

_____ equals _____ hundreds, _____ tens, and _____ ones.

6.

_____ equals _____ hundreds, _____ tens, and _____ ones.

7. **Number Sense** Complete the pattern.

100	200	300		500		700	800	900	

8. Use Tools Lucy picked a number. She says her number has 8 hundreds, 0 tens, and 0 ones.

What is Lucy's number?

_____

9. 🅰ᶻ **Vocabulary** Complete the sentences using the words below.

hundred   tens   ones

There are 100 _____ in one hundred.

There are 10 _____ in one _____.

Higher Order Thinking Farrah and Cory are playing beanbag toss.
Circle the two other numbers they each must get to score 1,000 points.

10. Farrah has 300 points.

200   500   600   300

11. Cory has 500 points.

100   200   400   700

12. 🌀 **Assessment Practice** Each box has 100 pencils. Count by hundreds to find the total. Which number tells how many pencils are in the boxes? 🐢 2.NBT.1.1.a

Ⓐ 170   Ⓒ 800

Ⓑ 700   Ⓓ 900

© Pearson Education, Inc. 2

Name _____

Solve & Share

How can you use place-value blocks to show 125? Explain.

Draw your blocks to show what you did.

I can ...
use place-value blocks and drawings to model and write 3-digit numbers.

MAFS.2.NBT.I.I Understand that the three digits of a three-digit number represent amounts of hundreds, tens, and ones. . . . Also 2.NBT.I.3
MAFS.K12.MP.I.I, MP.5.I

What number do the models show?

Remember, 10 ones make 1 ten.
10 tens make 1 hundred.

First, count the hundreds.

Use a **place-value chart** to show the value of each **digit**.

Hundreds	Tens	Ones
2		

Then count the tens.

Hundreds	Tens	Ones
2	5	

Then count the ones.

Hundreds	Tens	Ones
2	5	9

The models show 259. 259 has 3 digits.

Convince Me! How many hundreds are in 395? How many tens? How many ones?

☆ **Guided Practice** ☆ Write the numbers shown. Use place-value blocks and your workmat if needed.

1.

Hundreds	Tens	Ones
	7	0

70

2.

Hundreds	Tens	Ones

____

© Pearson Education, Inc. 2

Tools Assessment

Independent Practice ☆ Write the numbers shown. Use models and your workmat if needed.

3.

Hundreds	Tens	Ones

_____

4.

Hundreds	Tens	Ones

_____

5.

Hundreds	Tens	Ones

_____

6.

Hundreds	Tens	Ones

_____

7.

Hundreds	Tens	Ones

_____

8.

Hundreds	Tens	Ones

_____

9. Higher Order Thinking Find the number. It has 5 hundreds.
The digit in the tens place is between 5 and 7. The number of
ones is 2 less than 4. _____

10. Make Sense Complete the chart. A number has an 8 in the hundreds place. It does not have any tens. It has a 3 in the ones place. Check that your answer makes sense.

Hundreds	Tens	Ones

What is the number? _____

11. Draw models to show 1 hundred, 4 tens, and 3 ones. Then write the number in the chart.

Hundreds	Tens	Ones

12. Higher Order Thinking Choose a three-digit number.
Draw models to show the hundreds, tens, and ones for your number.
Write the number below.

_____

13. ⚑ **Assessment Practice** Katie used these models to show a number. Which number is shown?

Ⓐ 759

Ⓑ 768

Ⓒ 858

Ⓓ 859

© Pearson Education, Inc. 2

Name _____

Solve & Share

Jake says the 3 in 738 has a value of 3. He shows this with 3 ones blocks. Do you agree with Jake? Explain. Use the chart to help.

I can ...
tell the value of a digit by where it is placed in a number.

MAFS.2.NBT.1.1 Understand that the three digits of a three-digit number represent amounts of hundreds, tens, and ones. . . . Also 2.NBT.1.3
MAFS.K12.MP.4.1, MP.8.1

Hundreds	Tens	Ones

_____

_____

_____

_____

What is the value of each digit in 354?

You can build the number with blocks.

Remember, you can use a place-value chart to show the value of each digit.

Hundreds	Tens	Ones
3	5	4

The position of a digit tells its value.

354

The 3 has a value of 3 hundreds or 300.

The 5 has a value of 5 tens or 50.

The 4 has a value of 4 ones or 4.

Convince Me! How can you find the value of a digit using a place-value chart?

☆ **Guided Practice** ☆ Use place-value blocks to show the number. Next, complete the place-value chart. Then write the value of each digit.

I. 348

Hundreds	Tens	Ones
3	4	8

The ___3___ has a value of ___3___ hundreds or ___300___.

The ___4___ has a value of ___4___ tens or ___40___.

The ___8___ has a value of ___8___ ones or ___8___.

Topic 9 | Lesson 3

Independent Practice   Circle the correct values for the underlined digit in each number.

2.	17<u>3</u>	3	30	3 hundreds	3 ones	3 tens
3.	<u>4</u>39	4 tens	4 hundreds	4	40	400
4.	6<u>6</u>1	6 hundreds	60	6 tens	600	6 ones
5.	<u>5</u>18	500	5 tens	5 hundreds	5	50
6.	74<u>2</u>	20	200	2	2 tens	2 ones

7. Use the number to answer each question.

902

What is the value of the 9?

_____

What is the value of the 0?

_____

What is the value of the 2?

8. **Higher Order Thinking** Write the number that has the following values.

- The tens digit has a value of 70.

- The ones digit has a value of 5 ones.

- The hundreds digit has a value of 8 hundreds.

9. Complete the chart to find the number.

The number has 9 hundreds.
It has 5 tens.
It has 8 ones.

Hundreds	Tens	Ones

What is the number? _____

10. Model Courtney drew a picture of place-value blocks to show the number 793. Draw the blocks to show what Courtney's picture may have looked like.

11. Higher Order Thinking A class needs to build the number 123 with place-value blocks but does **NOT** have any hundreds blocks. How can they build 123 using other place-value blocks?

_____

_____

_____

12. 🅜 **Assessment Practice** What is the value of the 6 in the number 862? 🔵 2.NBT.1.1

- Ⓐ 6
- Ⓑ 10
- Ⓒ 60
- Ⓓ 600

© Pearson Education, Inc. 2

Name _____

Solve & Share

What is another way to write the number 231? Explain.

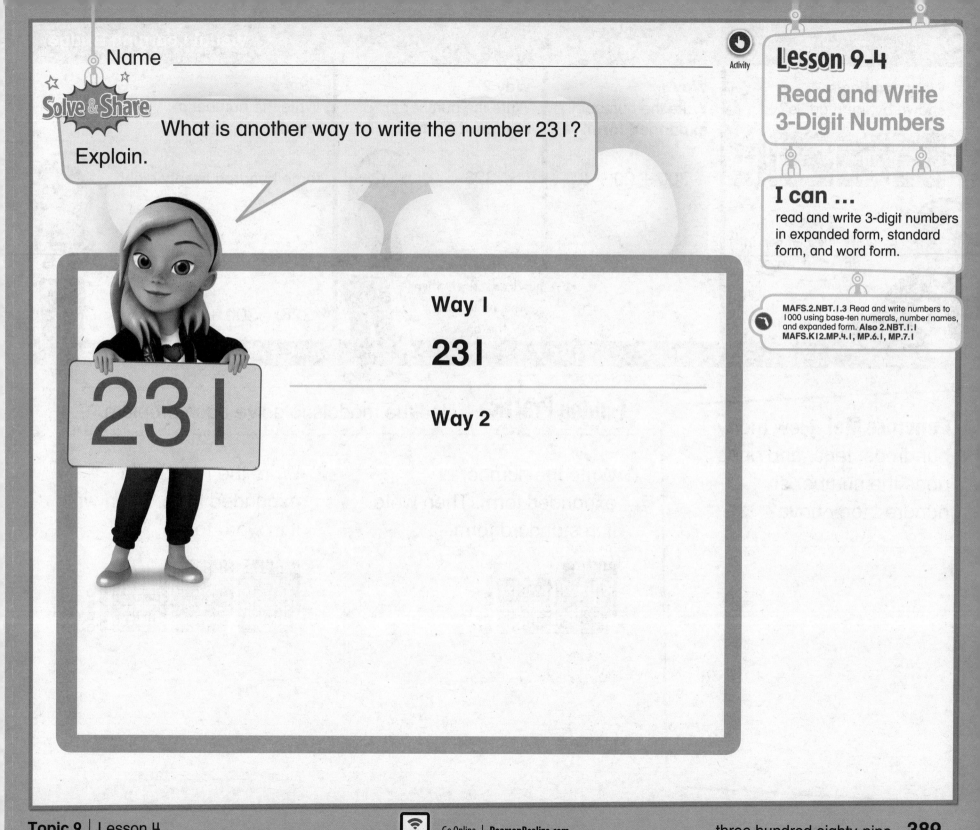

231

Way I

231

Way 2

I can ...

read and write 3-digit numbers in expanded form, standard form, and word form.

MAFS.2.NBT.1.3 Read and write numbers to 1000 using base-ten numerals, number names, and expanded form. **Also 2.NBT.1.1** MAFS.K12.MP.4.1, MP.6.1, MP.7.1

What number is shown by the models?

You can write the number in different ways.

Way 1
Write the number in **expanded form**.

$$300 + 20 + 8$$

Way 2
Write the number in **standard form**.

328

Write the hundreds first, then the tens, then the ones.

Way 3
Write the number in **word form**.

three hundred twenty-eight

All three ways show the same number!

$$328 = 300 + 20 + 8$$

Convince Me! How many hundreds, tens, and ones does the number six hundred forty have?

☆ **Guided Practice**   Use the models to solve each problem.

1. Write the number in expanded form. Then write it in standard form.

$$\underline{300} + \underline{5}$$

$$\underline{305}$$

2. Write the number in expanded form. Then write it in word form.

$$\underline{\hspace{2cm}} + \underline{\hspace{2cm}} + \underline{\hspace{2cm}}$$

$$\underline{\hspace{5cm}}$$

Tools   Assessment

Independent Practice ⭐ Write the number in word form and standard form.

3. 300 + 80 + 2

_____
_____

4. 200 + 6

You can use place-value blocks to help!

_____
_____

5. 600 + 90 + 5

_____
_____

6. 500 + 30 + 3

_____
_____

7. Write eight hundred seventy-four in expanded form and standard form.

_____
_____

8. Write 478 in expanded form and word form.

_____
_____

9. Higher Order Thinking Write the number in two different ways. It has 5 hundreds. The tens digit is 1 less than the hundreds digit. The ones digit is 2 more than the hundreds digit.

Standard form: _____   Expanded form: _____

Use place-value models to help you solve the problems below.

10. **Vocabulary** There are 493 pages in a book.

Write the number 493 in **expanded form**.

_____ + _____ + _____

Write the number 493 in **word form**.

_____

11. **Higher Order Thinking** Draw hundreds, tens, and ones to show a three-digit number. Next, write the number in expanded form. Then use the word form of the number in a sentence.

12. 🌐 **Assessment Practice** The model shows a three-digit number. Which is the standard form of the number? 🌐 2.NBT.1.3

Ⓐ 300 + 80 + 6   Ⓑ 386   Ⓒ 300 + 90 + 7   Ⓓ 397

© Pearson Education, Inc. 2   **Topic 9** | Lesson 4

Name _____

Solve & Share

Use place-value blocks. Show two ways to make 213. Then draw each way. Tell how your ways are alike and different.

Different Ways to Name the Same Number

Make your models here.

I can ...
make and name a number in different ways to show the same value.

MAFS.2.NBT.1.3 Read and write numbers to 1000 using base-ten numerals, number names, and expanded form. **Also 2.NBT.1.1.a** MAFS.K12.MP.2.1, MP.3.1, MP.6.1

Draw your models here.

Way 1	**Way 2**

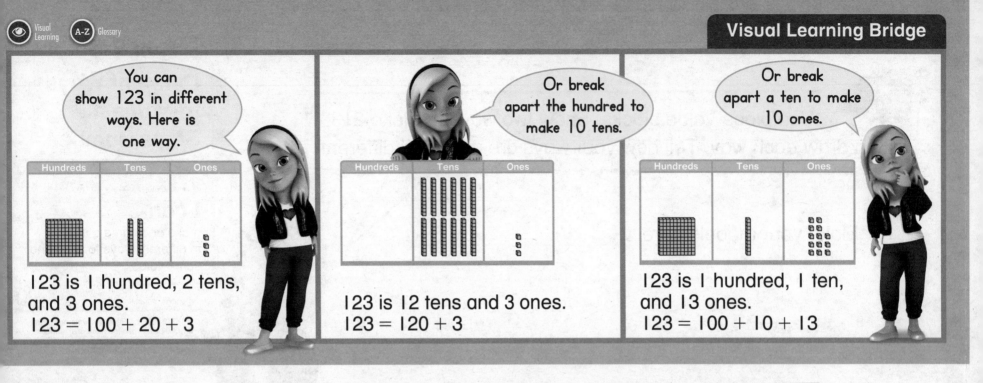

You can show 123 in different ways. Here is one way.

Hundreds	Tens	Ones

123 is 1 hundred, 2 tens, and 3 ones.
123 = 100 + 20 + 3

Or break apart the hundred to make 10 tens.

Hundreds	Tens	Ones

123 is 12 tens and 3 ones.
123 = 120 + 3

Or break apart a ten to make 10 ones.

Hundreds	Tens	Ones

123 is 1 hundred, 1 ten, and 13 ones.
123 = 100 + 10 + 13

Convince Me! How can you show that 5 hundreds and 4 tens has the same value as 4 hundreds and 14 tens?

☆ **Guided Practice** ☆ Use place-value blocks to count the hundreds, tens, and ones. Show two other ways to make the number.

1.

Hundreds	Tens	Ones

132 = 100 + 30 + 2

132 = _____

132 = _____

Name _____

Independent Practice

Use place-value blocks to count the hundreds, tens, and ones. Then show two other ways to make the number.

2.

Hundreds	Tens	Ones

418 = _____

418 = _____

418 = _____

3.

Hundreds	Tens	Ones

163 = _____

163 = _____

163 = _____

4.

Hundreds	Tens	Ones

225 = _____

225 = _____

225 = _____

Algebra Write the missing number.

5. $698 = 500 + \underline{\quad} + 8$

6. $939 = 900 + 20 + \underline{\quad}$

7. Carl made this model to show a number.

Hundreds	Tens	Ones

What number is shown? _____

Draw models to show another way
Carl could make this number.

8. Explain Neha wants to make the same number in different ways. She says 300 + 130 + 9 equals the same number as 500 + 30 + 9. Do you agree with Neha? Explain.

_____

_____

_____

Remember, you can show the same number in different ways.

9. Higher Order Thinking Make 572 as hundreds, tens, and ones. Write as many ways as you can.

_____

_____

_____

10. 🏴 **Assessment Practice** Which is a way to show 687? Choose all that apply. 🏴 2.NBT.1.3

☐ 600 + 70 + 17

☐ 600 + 80 + 7

☐ 600 + 180 + 7

☐ 500 + 180 + 7

Solve & Share

Write the missing numbers in the chart.
Be ready to explain how you found the missing numbers.

Lesson 9-6
Place-Value Patterns with Numbers

I can ...
use place-value patterns to mentally count by 1s and 10s from a given number.

MAFS.2.NBT.1.2 Count within 1000; skip-count by 5s, 10s, and 100s. Also 2.NBT.2.8
MAFS.K12.MP.7.1, MP.8.1

51	52	53	54	55	56	57	58	59	60
61	62	63	64	65	66	67	68	69	70
71	72	73	74	75	76	77	78	79	80
	82	83		85				89	
91			94		96	97	98		100
101	102	103	104	105	106	107	108	109	110
111	112	113	114	115	116	117	118	119	120
	122	123		125				129	
131			134				138		

You can use place-value patterns and mental math to count by 1s and 10s to 100.

37, 38, 39, 40, 41!

31	32	33	34	35	36	37
41	42	43	44	45	46	47
51	52	53	54	55	56	57

The ones digits go up by 1 from left to right.
The tens digits go up by 1 from top to bottom.

You can also use place-value patterns and mental math to count by 1s and 10s to 1,000.

537, 547, 557, 567!

531	532	533	534	535	536	537
541	542	543	544	545	546	547
551	552	553	554	555	556	557

The ones digits go up by 1 from left to right.
The tens digits go up by 1 from top to bottom.

Convince Me! Use mental math and place-value patterns to write each missing number.

538, 539, _____, 541, 542

481, 491, _____, 511, 521

☆ **Guided Practice** ☆ Use place-value patterns and mental math to find the missing numbers.

1.

784	785	786	787	788	789	790
794	795	796	797	798	799	800
804	805	806	807	808	809	810

2.

412		414		416		418
422			425		427	
432	433		435	436	437	

Topic 9 | Lesson 6

Name _____

Tools Assessment

Independent Practice

Use place-value patterns and mental math to find the missing numbers.

3.

884			887		889
	895			898	
904	905		907	908	

4.

	146	147			150
155				159	
	166	167		169	170

5. 456, 457, 458, _____, _____,

461, 462, _____, _____, _____

6. 620, 630, 640, _____, 660, _____,

680, 690, _____, 710, _____

7. 232, 242, _____, 262, _____,

_____, 292, 302, _____, _____

8. 991, 992, _____, _____, 995,

_____, 997, _____, 999, _____

Number Sense Describe each number pattern.

9. 130 → 230 → 330 → 430 → 530

_____

10. 320 → 330 → 340 → 350 → 360

_____

11. **Look for Patterns** Sally sees a pattern in these numbers. Describe the pattern.

> 995, 996, 997, 998, 999, 1,000

_____

_____

_____

12. **Look for Patterns** Yoshi sees a pattern in these numbers. Describe the pattern.

> 341, 351, 361, 371, 381, 391

_____

_____

_____

13. **Higher Order Thinking** Write your own three-digit numbers. Describe the number pattern for your numbers.

_____, _____, _____, _____, _____

_____

_____

14. 🐊 **Assessment Practice** Use the numbers on the cards. Write the missing numbers in the number chart. 🐊 2.NBT.1.2

| 222 | 214 | 224 | 231 |

210	211	212	213		215
220	221		223		225
230		232	233	234	235

Name _____

Solve & Share

Use the number line to skip count by 5s, starting at 0. Write the two missing numbers. Describe any patterns you see.

I can ...
skip count by 5s, 10s, and 100s using a number line.

MAFS.2.NBT.1.2 Count within 1000;
skip-count by 5s, 10s, and 100s.
Also 2.NBT.2.8
MAFS.K12.MP.2.1, MP.7.1, MP.8.1

0   5   10   15   20   [ ]   [ ]

_____

_____

_____

This number line shows skip counting by 5s.

I see a pattern in the ones digits!

400 405 410 415 420 425 430

This number line shows skip counting by 100s.

I see a pattern in the hundreds digits!

400 500 600 700 800 900 1,000

Convince Me! How could you use the number line in the first box above to skip count by 10s starting at 400?

✩ **Guided Practice** ✩   Skip count on the number line. Write the missing numbers.

1.

570   580   590   [600]   [610]   620   [630]   [640]   650

2.

      100   300   600   800

[ ]   [ ]   [ ]   [ ]   [ ]

Topic 9 | Lesson 7

Tools   Assessment

Independent Practice   Skip count on the number line.
Write the missing numbers.

3.
20 [ ] 40 50 [ ] [ ] 80 [ ] 100 110 [ ] 130 140

4.
820 825 830 [ ] [ ] 845 [ ] [ ]

> You can skip count by 5s, 10s, or 100s.

Look at the skip counting pattern. Write the missing numbers.

5. 100, 200, 300, 400, _____, _____

6. 950, 960, _____, 980, 990, _____

7. 480, 490, 500, _____, _____, 530

8. 745, 750, _____, _____, 765, _____

9. Algebra Write the missing numbers.

300 + _____ = 400   85 + _____ = 90   990 + _____ = 1,000

10. **Reasoning** Greg is skip counting. He writes 430, 435, 440 on paper. Greg wants to write 3 more numbers after 440. What should they be?

_____ , _____ , _____

11. **Reasoning** Zoe is skip counting. She writes 500, 600, 700 on paper. Zoe wants to write 3 more numbers after 700. What should they be?

_____ , _____ , _____

12. **Higher Order Thinking** What number is used to skip count on this number line? How do you know? What numbers did the arrows land on at the jumps?

300   310   320   330   340

13. 🔘 **Assessment Practice** Roy played 4 video games. He scored 110, 115, 120, and 125 points.

Skip counting by what number from 110 to 125 is shown on the number line? 🔘 2.NBT.1.2

110   115   120   125

Ⓐ 2   Ⓑ 5   Ⓒ 10   Ⓓ 100

☆ ☆
Solve & Share

Joy and Zach flipped three number cards. Then they each made a number. Joy made 501 and Zach made 510.

Who made the greater number? How do you know? Use place-value blocks to help you solve.

I can ...
compare numbers using place value.

MAFS.2.NBT.1.4 Compare two three-digit numbers based on meanings of the hundreds, tens, and ones digits, using >, =, and < symbols to record the results of comparisons. **Also 2.NBT.1.1**
MAFS.K12.MP.2.1, MP.3.1, MP.8.1

Hundreds	Tens	Ones

_____ is greater than _____.

Use place-value blocks to show each number. To compare the numbers, start with the digit that has the greatest place value.

Compare 325 and 225.

Hundreds	Tens	Ones
3	2	5
2	2	5

Compare the hundreds first.

300 is **greater than** 200.

So, 325 ⬭> 225.

Compare 736 and 756.

Hundreds	Tens	Ones
7	3	6
7	5	6

If the hundreds are equal, compare the tens.

30 is **less than** 50.

So, 736 ⬭< 756.

Compare 897 and 897.

Hundreds	Tens	Ones
8	9	7
8	9	7

The hundreds, the tens, and the ones are **equal**.

897 is equal to 897.

So, 897 ⬭= 897.

Convince Me! How would you compare 995 and 890? Explain.

Guided Practice Use place-value blocks to show each number. Compare. Write greater than, less than, or equal to. Then write >, <, or =.

1. 264 is _greater than_ 178.

   264 ⬭> 178

Hundreds	Tens	Ones
2	6	4
1	7	8

2. 816 is _____ 819.

   816 ◯ 819

Hundreds	Tens	Ones

© Pearson Education, Inc. 2

Topic 9 | Lesson 8

Independent Practice

Use place-value blocks to show each number. Compare. Write greater than, less than, or equal to. Then write >, <, or =.

3.

572 is _____ 577.

572 ◯ 577

4.

256 is _____ 243.

256 ◯ 243

5.

837 is _____ 837.

837 ◯ 837

6.

486 is _____ 468.

486 ◯ 468

7.

208 is _____ 208.

208 ◯ 208

8.

936 is _____ 836.

936 ◯ 836

9.

821 is _____ 821.

821 ◯ 821

10.

347 is _____ 437.

347 ◯ 437

11.

286 is _____ 189.

286 ◯ 189

12. Higher Order Thinking Find one number that will make all three comparisons true.

_____ < 111   _____ > 109   _____ = 110

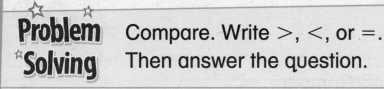

Problem Solving

Compare. Write >, <, or =.
Then answer the question.

---

13. Reasoning Ming sells 319 tickets. Josie sells 315 tickets. Who sells more tickets?

How can you use symbols to relate the numbers?

319 ◯ 315

_____ sells more tickets.

14. Reasoning Jared earned 189 pennies doing chores. Tara earned 200 pennies doing chores. Who earned more pennies?

189 ◯ 200

_____ earned more pennies.

---

15. Higher Order Thinking Compare the numbers 298 and 289. Write the comparison two ways. Then explain your thinking.

_____ ◯ _____

_____ ◯ _____

_____

_____

_____

16. **Assessment Practice** Solve the riddle to find the number of coins in the second chest. Then compare the numbers.

The two numbers have the same digits.
The hundreds digits are the same.
The tens and ones digits are in different orders. **2.NBT.1.4**

556 coins

? coins

Ⓐ 556 < 665

Ⓑ 556 > 565

Ⓒ 556 = 565

Ⓓ 556 < 565

---

408 four hundred eight

© Pearson Education, Inc. 2

Topic 9 | Lesson 8

Name _____

Solve & Share

This number line shows only one number.
Name a number that is greater than 256. Then, name
a number that is less than 256. Show your numbers
on the number line and explain why you are correct.

I can ...
compare and write a three-
digit number that is greater
than or less than another
three-digit number.

MAFS.2.NBT.1.4 Compare two three-digit
numbers based on meanings of the hundreds,
tens, and ones digits, using >, =, and <
symbols to record the results of comparisons.
Also 2.NBT.1.1
MAFS.K12.MP.2.1, MP.7.1, MP.8.1

←————————————|————————————→
                    256

_____ is greater than 256.

_____ is less than 256.

○ Visual Learning   (A-Z) Glossary

You can write numbers that are greater than or less than another number, using a number line.

324 < 325

On a number line, the numbers to the left are less. 323 and 324 are both less than 325.

324 is less than 325.

327 > 325

On a number line, the numbers to the right are greater. 326 and 327 are both greater than 325.

327 is greater than 325.

325 > 323
325 < 326

325 is greater than 323 and less than 326.

Convince Me! Can you write a number that is less than 325, and that is not shown on the number line above? Explain.

☆ **Guided Practice** ☆   Write a number to make each comparison correct. Draw a number line to help if needed.

1. _461_ < 467

2. _____ < 470

3. 132 < _____

4. 263 < _____

5. 675 > _____

6. 684 = _____

Independent Practice   Write a number to make each comparison correct. Draw a number line to help if needed.

7. 421 > _____

8. _____ < 884

9. 959 < _____

10. _____ < 619

11. 103 = _____

12. 566 > _____

13. 394 < _____

14. _____ < 417

15. _____ > 789

Write <, >, or = to make each comparison correct.

16. 107 ◯ 106

17. 630 ◯ 629

18. 832 ◯ 832

19. **Higher Order Thinking** Write a number to make each comparison correct. Place the numbers on the number lines.

_____ < 780 < _____

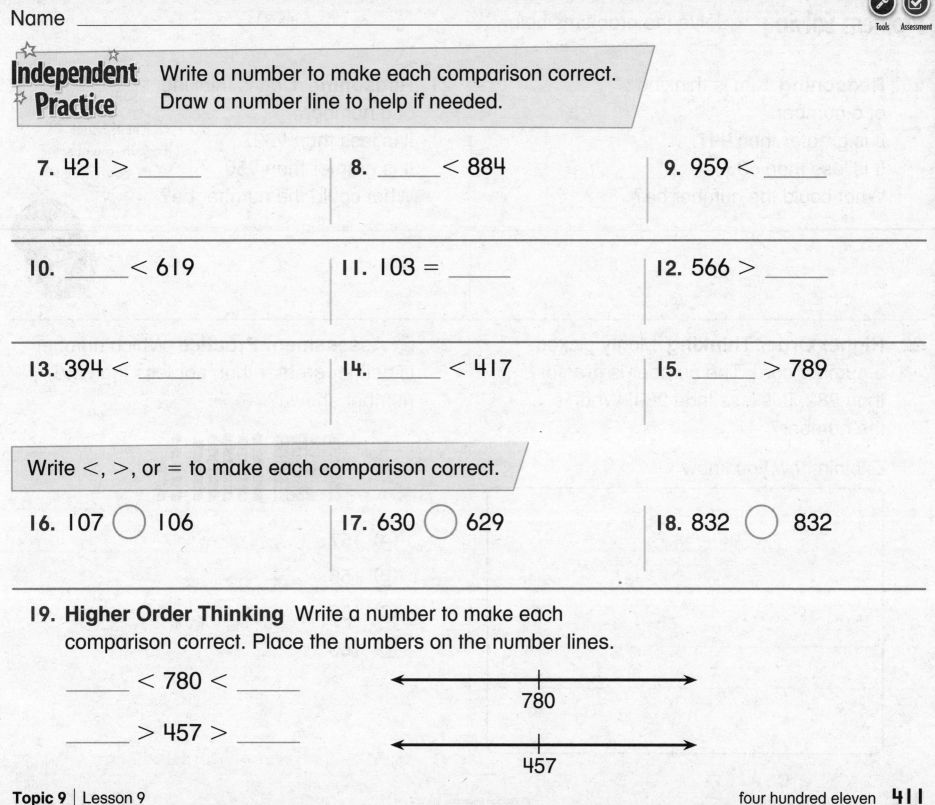

780

_____ > 457 > _____

457

20. Reasoning Kim is thinking of a number.
It is greater than 447.
It is less than 635.
What could the number be?

_____

21. Reasoning Don is thinking of a number.
It is less than 982.
It is greater than 950.
What could the number be?

Think about how the numbers relate.

_____

22. Higher Order Thinking Monty picked a number card. The number is greater than 282. It is less than 284. What is the number? _____

Explain how you know.

23. 🅕 **Assessment Practice** Which number is neither greater than nor less than the number shown?   2.NBT.1.4

Ⓐ 157

Ⓑ 158

Ⓒ 159

Ⓓ 168

© Pearson Education, Inc. 2

Name _____

Solve & Share

Sort the numbers 500, 800, 600, 400, and 700 from least to greatest.
Describe any number patterns that you see.
Are there any other numbers that fit the pattern?

[ ] [ ] [ ] [ ] [ ]

Number patterns

I can ...
look for patterns to help me solve problems.

MAFS.K12.MP.7.1 Look for and use structure.
Also MP.1.1, MP.2.1, MP.3.1
MAFS.2.NBT.1.2 Count within 1000; skip-count by 5s, 10s, and 100s. Also 2.NBT.2.8, 2.NBT.1.4

Thinking Habits

Are there things in common that help me?

Is there a pattern? How does it help?

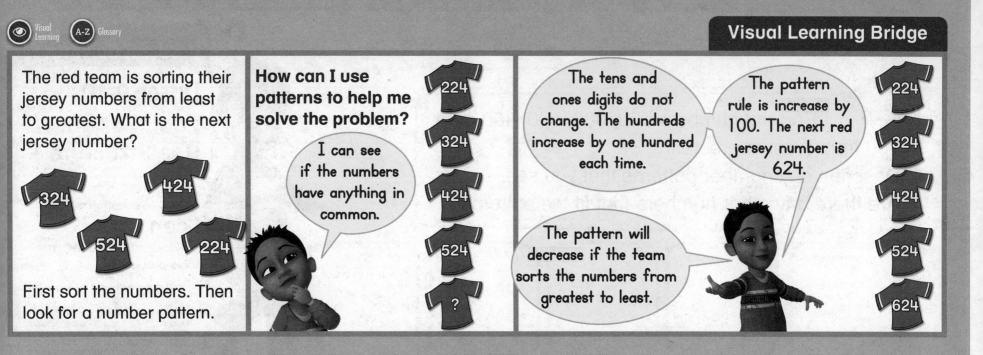

Convince Me! How can you use the pattern to find the next three red jersey numbers?

☆ **Guided Practice**   Look for a pattern to solve each problem.

1. The yellow team is sorting their uniforms.

    420   440   410   430   ?

    Sort the first four jersey numbers from least to greatest.

    _____, _____, _____, _____

2. Look for a pattern in the sorted jersey numbers. What is the pattern rule?

    _____

3. What is the next greatest yellow jersey number? _____

Independent Practice Break the problem into simpler parts to solve. Use a hundreds chart, a number line, or place value chart if you need to.

4. The blue team wants to sort their jersey numbers from greatest to least. After they sort the numbers, what number would come next?

List the jersey numbers from greatest to least.

_____ , _____ , _____ , _____

Compare two numbers at a time to help you put the numbers in order.

Look for a pattern in the sorted jersey numbers. What is the pattern rule?

_____

What jersey number is next in the pattern?

_____

5. A librarian sorted these books. Find the missing book number. _____

Describe one pattern you notice.

_____

_____

_____

Problem Solving

Mail Delivery

Sam delivered mail to four houses numbered 115, 120, 110, and 105. He started at the house with the least number and continued to the house with the greatest number.

If the number pattern continues, what are the next three house numbers?

6. **Reasoning** Sort the numbers of the first four houses from least to greatest. Then write the sorted numbers on the houses in the top row above. 🐾 2.NBT.1.2, 2.NBT.1.4, MP.2.1

_____

7. **Look for Patterns** What is the pattern rule for the four house numbers you sorted? 🐾 2.NBT.1.2, MP.7.1

_____

_____

What are the next three house numbers?

_____

Write the numbers of the houses in the bottom row of houses above.

8. **Explain** Why do you sort the numbers before looking for a pattern? Explain. 🐾 MP.3.1

_____

_____

Follow the Path

Color a path from **Start** to **Finish**. Follow the sums and differences that are even numbers. You can only move up, down, right, or left.

Start								
66 − 28	15 + 12	64 − 27	57 + 36	99 − 66	53 − 14	23 + 46	75 − 22	52 + 13
15 + 35	59 − 28	57 + 22	87 − 74	56 − 12	78 − 52	61 + 15	42 − 29	29 + 16
53 + 43	44 + 39	90 − 18	47 − 23	61 + 39	61 − 36	24 + 38	15 + 58	73 − 52
85 − 39	56 + 17	43 − 11	25 + 26	81 − 28	61 + 14	53 − 37	33 + 38	45 − 18
33 + 57	78 − 52	56 + 12	87 − 32	16 + 45	93 − 24	63 + 15	26 + 44	27 − 19

Finish

Vocabulary Review

Word List
- compare
- decrease
- digits
- equals (=)
- expanded form
- greater than (>)
- hundred
- increase
- less than (<)
- ones
- place-value chart
- standard form
- tens
- thousand
- word form

Understand Vocabulary

Write *standard form*, *expanded form*, or *word form*.

1. 400 + 30 + 7

2. four hundred thirty-seven

3. 437

Label each picture. Use terms from the Word List.

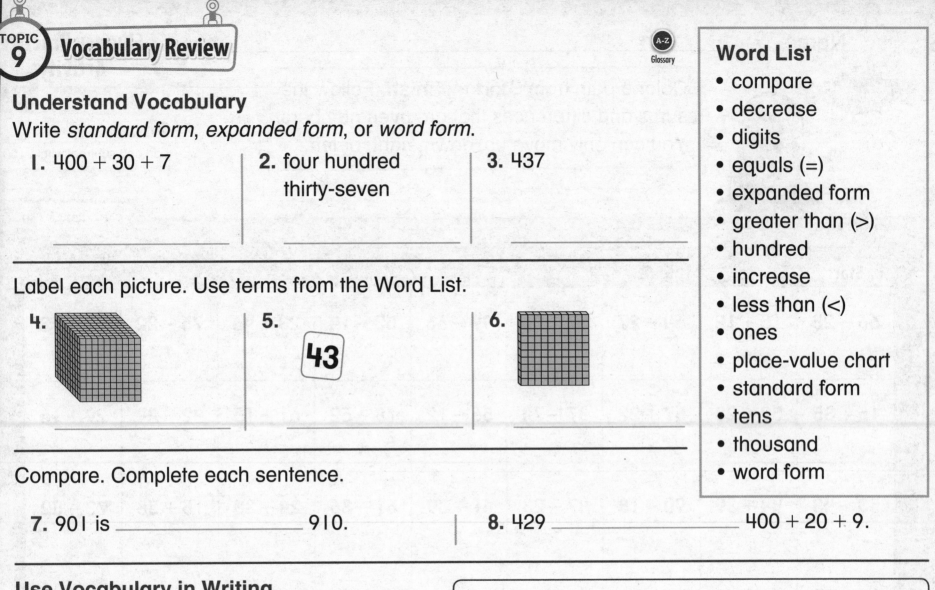

4.

5. 43

6.

Compare. Complete each sentence.

7. 901 is _____ 910.

8. 429 _____ 400 + 20 + 9.

Use Vocabulary in Writing

9. What is the next number in the pattern?
911, 921, 931, 941, _____

Explain how you solved the problem.
Use terms from the Word List.

Name _____

Set A

10 tens make 1 hundred.
You can count by hundreds.

_700_ equals _7_ hundreds,

_0_ tens, and _0_ ones.

Complete the sentence.
Use models if needed.

1.

_____ equals _____ hundreds,

_____ tens, and _____ ones.

Set B

You can use place value to help
you write numbers.

Hundreds	Tens	Ones
3	2	4

324

There are 3 hundreds, 2 tens,
and 4 ones in 324.

Write the numbers. Use models and
your workmat if needed.

2.

Hundreds	Tens	Ones

_____

3.

Hundreds	Tens	Ones

_____

You can write a number using the standard form, expanded form, and word form.

$\underline{215}$

$\underline{200} + \underline{10} + \underline{5}$

two hundred fifteen

Write the number in standard form, expanded form, and word form.

4.

$\underline{}$

$\underline{} + \underline{} + \underline{}$

$\underline{}$

You can show different ways to make numbers.

Hundreds	Tens	Ones

$238 = \underline{200} + \underline{30} + \underline{8}$

$238 = \underline{200} + \underline{20} + \underline{18}$

$238 = \underline{230} + \underline{8}$

Look at the models in the chart.
Show three different ways to make the number.

5.

Hundreds	Tens	Ones

$153 = \underline{} + \underline{} + \underline{}$

$153 = \underline{} + \underline{} + \underline{}$

$153 = \underline{} + \underline{}$

Name _____

Set E

You can look for patterns with numbers on a hundreds chart.

342	343	344	345	346	347
352	353	354	355	356	357
362	363	364	365	366	367

From left to right, the __ones__ digit goes up by 1.

From top to bottom, the __tens__ digit goes up by 1.

Set F

You can skip count by 5s, 10s, and 100s on a number line.

200   300 |400| |500| 600

Use place-value patterns to find the missing numbers.

6.

574		576	577	578	
584		586		588	589
	595	596	597		

7.

	222		224	225	
	232		234	235	236
241	242		244		246

Skip count on the number line. Write the missing numbers.

8.

95   100   110   125

You can use place value to compare numbers.

325   332

The hundreds are equal, so compare the tens. _20_ is less than _30_.

So, 325 (<) 332.

Compare each pair of numbers. Write >, <, or =.

9. 785 ◯ 793   **10.** 199 ◯ 198

11. 452 ◯ 452   **12.** 805 ◯ 810

13. 902 ◯ 897   **14.** 451 ◯ 516

15. 636 ◯ 629   **16.** 754 ◯ 754

Thinking Habits

Look For and Use Structure

Are there things in common that help me?

Is there a pattern? How does it help?

Look for a pattern to solve the problem.

17. These tags are in a drawer.

Describe a pattern you notice.

_____

_____

What is the missing number? _____

© Pearson Education, Inc. 2

Name _____

1. Each box has 100 crayons.
Count by hundreds to find the total.
How many crayons are in all of the
boxes? Explain.

_____

_____

_____

_____

2. Danny made this model.
Write the number in three
different forms.

Standard form _____

Expanded form _____

Word form _____

_____

3. Write the number the model shows.
Use the chart.

Hundreds	Tens	Ones

4. What is the value of the 8 in the number
789? What is the expanded form of 789?

_____

_____

_____

5. Which is the word form of the number shown by the blocks?

Ⓐ four hundred fifty-six

Ⓑ four hundred forty-six

Ⓒ 400 + 40 + 6

Ⓓ 446

6. Which is the standard form of the number shown by the blocks?

Ⓐ 315

Ⓑ three hundred fifteen

Ⓒ 300 + 10 + 5

Ⓓ 351

---

7. Draw a line from each number form to its example.

word form   standard form   expanded form

100 + 20 + 1   one hundred twenty-one   121

---

8. Kate made this model. What number does it show? Write the number and complete the sentence.

_____ equals _____ hundreds, _____ tens, and _____ ones.

© Pearson Education, Inc. 2

Topic 9 | Assessment Practice

9. Lee and Maria collect pennies.
Lee has 248 pennies.
Maria has 253 pennies.
Who has more pennies?

_____

Write <, =, or > to compare
the number of pennies.

248 ◯ 253

10. Jeff is thinking of a number.
The number has 2 hundreds.
It has more ones than tens.
It has 7 tens.

Which could be the number?
Choose all that apply.

☐ 276   ☐ 279   ☐ 267

☐ 278   ☐ 289

11. Compare. Write <, =, or >.

429 ◯ 294   849 ◯ 984

12. Write a number that will make each
comparison correct.

327 < _____   716 > _____

13. There are 326 boys at a school. Which is the expanded form for the number of boys?

Ⓐ 200 + 30 + 6   Ⓑ 300 + 20 + 6   Ⓒ 300 + 60 + 2   Ⓓ 300 + 60 + 7

14. Which is a way to show 576? Choose all that apply.

☐ 500 + 60 + 16   ☐ 500 + 70 + 6   ☐ 500 + 6

☐ 400 + 170 + 6   ☐ 500 + 60 + 7

15. Use the numbers on the cards.
Write the missing numbers in the
number chart.

320		322	323	324
330		332		334
	341	342	343	344

16. Candy counts 405, 410, 415, 420, 425, 430.
By what number does Candy skip count?

Ⓐ 2

Ⓑ 5

Ⓒ 10

Ⓓ 100

17. Skip count on the number line.
Write the missing numbers.

255   265   275

18. Choose all the comparisons that are
correct.

☐ $576 < 675$

☐ $899 < 799$

☐ $435 > 354$

☐ $698 < 896$

☐ $856 > 859$

Topic 9 | Assessment Practice

Name _____

Reading Record

These students love to read!
These books show the number of pages
each student has read so far this year.

I. Write the number of pages Tim read
in expanded form. 2.NBT.1.1, 2.NBT.1.3, MP.7.1

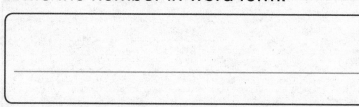

_____ + _____ + _____

Write the number in word form.

_____

2. Complete the place-value chart
to show the number of pages
Ruth read.

Hundreds	Tens	Ones

Show two other ways to write the number.

2.NBT.1.1, 2.NBT.1.3, MP.7.1

_____ + _____ + _____

_____ + _____ + _____

3. Show two ways to compare the number of pages
that Luisa read with the number of pages that
Ruth read. Use > and <. 2.NBT.1.4, MP.2.1

_____ ◯ _____

_____ ◯ _____

4. This number line shows the total number of minutes Diane read each week for 3 weeks.

0   100   200   300

How many minutes did she read after the first week? _____ minutes

After the second week? _____ minutes

After the third week? _____ minutes

How many minutes did she read each week? Explain how you know.
2.NBT.1.2, MP.3.1, MP.7.1

[ ]

5. Diane reads the same number of minutes each week. How many minutes does she read after 4 weeks? After 5 weeks? Skip count on the number line above to find the answers. 2.NBT.1.2, 2.NBT.2.8, MP.7.1

After 4 weeks: _____ minutes

After 5 weeks: _____ minutes

6. The table shows how many pages Jim read in three different months. If he follows the pattern, how many pages will Jim read in April and May?
2.NBT.1.2, 2.NBT.2.8, MP.7.1

Number of Pages Read	
January	210
February	220
March	230
April	?
May	?

Part A
What pattern do you see in the table?

[ ]

Part B
How many pages will Jim read in April and May?

[ ]

© Pearson Education, Inc. 2

Topic 9 | Performance Task

Add Within 1,000 Using Models and Strategies

Essential Question: What are strategies for adding numbers to 1,000?

Digital Resources

Interactive Student Edition · Activity · Visual Learning · Video · Practice

Assessment · Games · Tools · Glossary

MAFS.2.NBT.2.7, 2.NBT.2.8, 2.NBT.2.9, 2.MD.3.8,

MAFS.K12.MP.1.1, MP.2.1, MP.3.1, MP.4.1, MP.5.1, MP.6.1, MP.7.1, MP.8.1

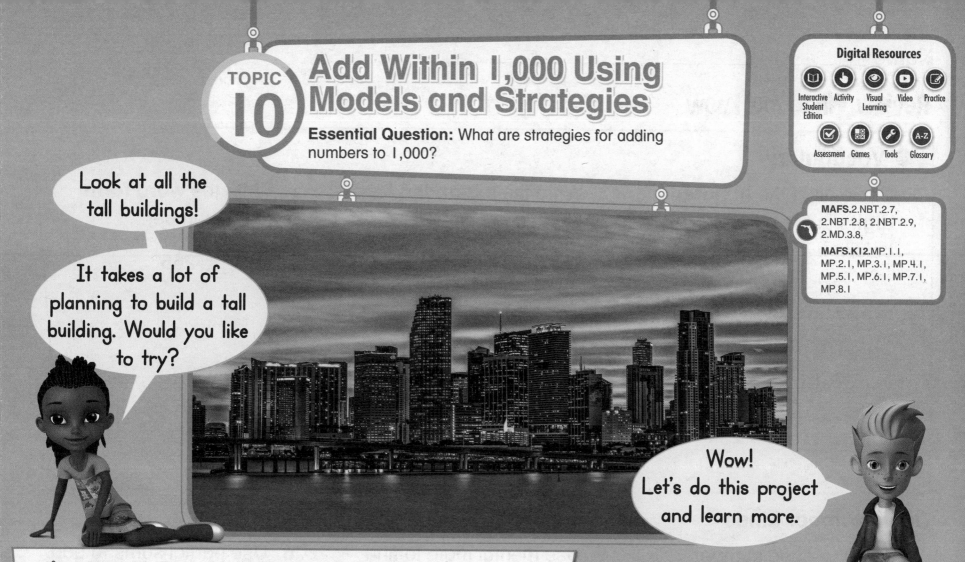

Look at all the tall buildings!

It takes a lot of planning to build a tall building. Would you like to try?

Wow! Let's do this project and learn more.

enVision® STEM Project: Building Up to 1,000

Find Out Use drinking straws and pieces of tape. The total number of straws and pieces of tape cannot be more than 1,000. First, decide how many of each to use. Then share. Build the tallest buildings you can.

Journal: Make a Book Describe your building in a book. In your book, also:

- Tell how many drinking straws and pieces of tape you used.

- Tell how you would make a better building if you did it again.

Name _____

A-Z Vocabulary

1. Circle all of the **hundreds digits** in the numbers below.

   5 0 2

   5 8

   1,0 0 0

2. Write the **expanded form** of the number.

   846

   _____

3. Write the **word form** of the number.

   265

   _____

   _____

Open Number Lines

4. Use the open number line to find the sum.

   ⟵——————————⟶

   54 + 13 = _____

Mental Math

5. Use mental math to find each sum.

   40 + 37 = _____

   6 + 77 + 4 = _____

Partial Sums

6. Use partial sums to add.

   $\begin{array}{r} 46 \\ +53 \\ \hline \end{array}$ $\begin{array}{r} 29 \\ +61 \\ \hline \end{array}$

Name _____

PROJECT 10A

What are the run times of two of your favorite movies?

Project: Write Movie Reviews

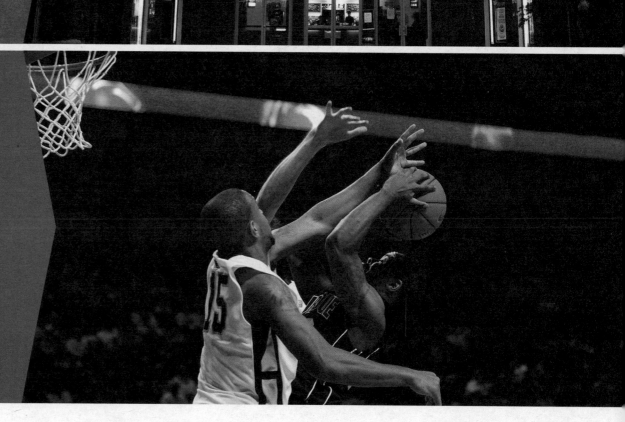

PROJECT 10B

How many shots do basketball teams block?

Project: Make a Basketball Poster

How many miles are between Tallahassee and other cities?

Project: Draw a Florida Map

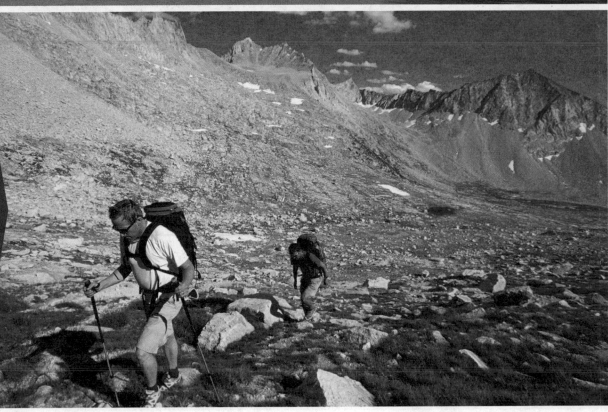

How far can people hike in the Sierra Nevada Mountains?

Project: Create a Hiking Guide

© Pearson Education, Inc. 2

Name _____

Solve & Share

Forest Park Nursery sells trees.
Sal buys a maple tree for $125.
A spruce tree costs $10 more than a maple tree.
An elm tree costs $100 more than a maple tree.
What is the cost of a spruce tree? An elm tree?

Use dollar bills, place-value blocks, or mental math to solve.
Be ready to explain how you solved the problem.

I can ...
add 10 and 100 mentally using
what I know about place value.

MAFS.2.NBT.2.8 Mentally add 10 or 100
to a given number 100–900, and mentally
subtract 10 or 100 from a given number
100–900. **Also 2.NBT.2.9, 2.MD.3.8**
MAFS.K12.MP.3.1, MP.4.1, MP.7.1

You can use mental math to add 10 or 100 to three-digit numbers.

Find 243 + 10.
Find 243 + 100.

How can I add 10 or 100 mentally?

243

243 + 10 = ?

Add 1 ten

4 tens plus 1 ten equals 5 tens.

So, 243 + 10 = 253.

243 + 100 = ?

Add 1 hundred

2 hundreds plus 1 hundred equals 3 hundreds.

So, 243 + 100 = 343.

Sometimes adding 10 changes the tens and hundreds digits.

Find 290 + 10.

I know 290 = 29 tens. 29 tens plus 1 ten equals 30 tens or 300. So, 290 + 10 = 300.

Convince Me! Use mental math to find 567 + 10 and 567 + 100. Explain your reasoning.

☆ **Guided Practice** ☆ Add. Use place-value blocks or mental math.

1. 325 + 10 = 335

2. ___ + ___ = ___

3. ___ + ___ = ___

4. ___ + ___ = ___

© Pearson Education, Inc. 2

Topic 10 | Lesson 1

Tools Assessment

Independent Practice ☆ Add. Use place-value blocks or mental math.

5. $164 + 100 =$ _____

6. $\$837 + \$10 =$ _____

7. $329 + 100 =$ _____

8. $610 + 10 =$ _____

9. $295 + 10 =$ _____

10. $\$497 + \$100 =$ _____

11. $790 + 10 =$ _____

12. $693 + 100 =$ _____

13. $900 + 100 =$ _____

14. $460 + 10 =$ _____

15. $185 + 10 =$ _____

16. $723 + 100 =$ _____

Algebra Find the missing numbers. Use mental math to solve.

17. $572 + \boxed{} = 672$

18. $285 + \boxed{} = 385$

19. $709 = 699 + \boxed{}$

20. $422 = 322 + \boxed{}$

21. $615 + \boxed{} = 625$

22. $600 = \boxed{} + 590$

23. **enVision® STEM** The Science Club asked 178 people about recycling. The club wants to ask a total of 188 people about recycling.

    How many more people will the Science Club need to ask?

    _____ more people

24. **Use Structure** Jordan has four $100 bills, three $20 bills, one $10 bill, and seven $1 bills. What will Jordan's total be if Jayla gives him one more $10 bill? What will his total be if she gives him one more $100 bill?

    _____

    _____

    Is there a shortcut that makes sense?

25. **Higher Order Thinking** Think of a 3-digit number. Write a story about adding 100 to your number. Then write an equation to show your solution.

    _____

    _____

    _____

    _____

    _____ + _____ = _____

26. 🐦 **Assessment Practice** Which equations are true? Choose all that apply. 🦃 2.NBT.2.8

    ☐ $251 + $10 = $351

    ☐ 528 + 100 = 628

    ☐ 528 + 10 = 538

    ☐ $251 + $100 = $351

© Pearson Education, Inc. 2   **Topic 10** | Lesson 1

Solve & Share

Use the open number line to find 598 + 123. Explain your work.

Lesson 10-2
Add on an Open Number Line

I can ...
use an open number line to add 3-digit numbers.

MAFS.2.NBT.2.7 Add and subtract within 1000, using concrete models or drawings and strategies . . . ; relate the strategy to a written method. Understand that in adding or subtracting three-digit numbers, one adds or subtracts hundreds and hundreds, tens and tens, ones and ones; and sometimes it is necessary to compose or decompose tens or hundreds. **Also 2.NBT.2.9**
MAFS.K12.MP.2.1, MP.4.1, MP.5.1

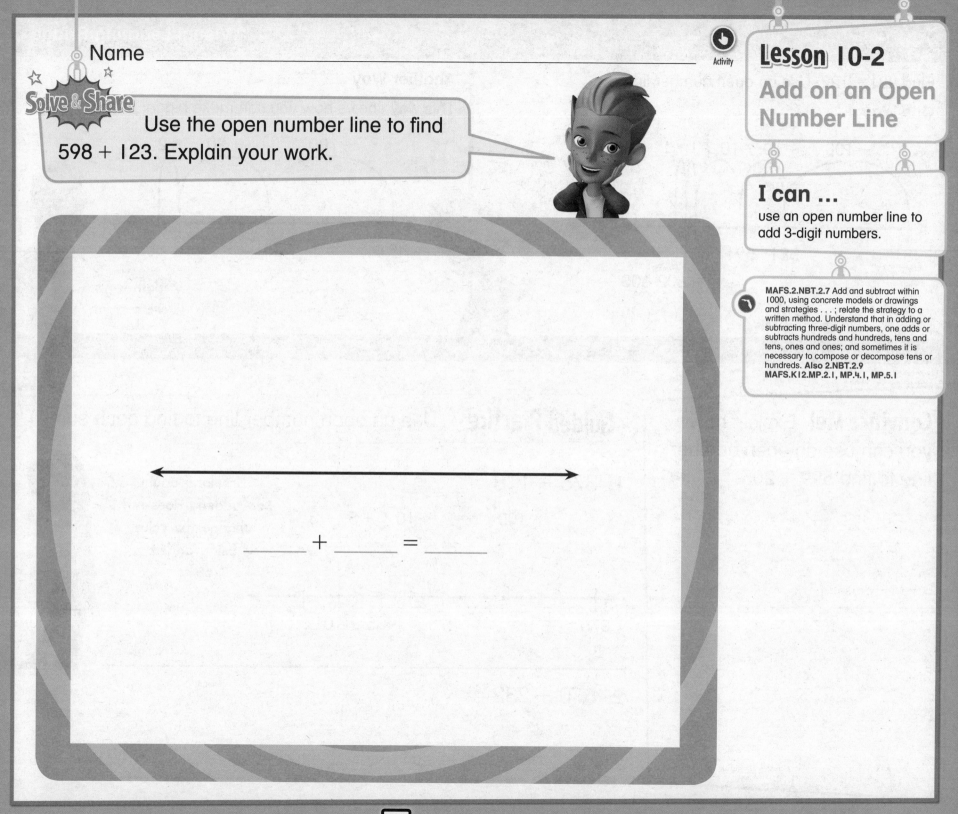

_____ + _____ = _____

Find 481 + 122. Use an open number line.
One Way

+100 +10 +10 +1 +1

481   581 591 601
602 603

This way shows jumps by 100s, 10s, and 1s.

481 + 122 = 603

Another Way

This way shows how you can make bigger jumps.

+100   +20 +2

481   581   601 603

Both ways are correct.

Convince Me! Explain how you can use an open number line to find 599 + 205.

☆ **Guided Practice**   Use an open number line to find each sum.

1. 375 + 118 = _____

+100   +10 +5 +3

375   475 485 490 493

Breaking apart an addend does not change the value being added.

2. 670 + 232 = _____

© Pearson Education, Inc. 2

Topic 10 | Lesson 2

Name _____

Independent Practice ☆ Use an open number line to find each sum.

3. 269 + 156 = _____

4. 637 + 242 = _____

5. 886 + 114 = _____

6. 208 + 598 = _____

7. Higher Order Thinking Lisa finds 550 + 298 using the open number line below.
Is her work correct? Explain.

+ 100   + 100   + 100
                              − 2

550   650   750   848 850

_____

_____

_____

_____

_____

8. **Reasoning** José has 181 cards. He collects 132 more cards. How many cards does he have now?

⟵————————————————————⟶

_____ cards

9. (A-Z) **Vocabulary** Complete the sentence using two of these terms.

add   tens   open number line   rule

An _____

can be used to _____.

---

10. **Higher Order Thinking** Use open number lines to find $446 + 215$ in two different ways.

$446 + 215 =$ _____

⟵————————————————⟶   ⟵————————————————⟶

---

11. 🔴 **Assessment Practice** Mary uses an open number line to find $286 + 137$. All of the jumps she draws are greater than 1. Draw what Mary could have done. Write the sum. 🔵 2.NBT.2.7

$286 + 137 =$ _____

⟵————————————————⟶

Name _____

Use place-value blocks to find 243 + 354.
Tell which place value you added first and why.
Then draw a picture to show your work.

I can ...

use models to add 3-digit numbers and then explain my work.

MAFS.2.NBT.2.7 Add and subtract within 1000, using concrete models or drawings and strategies . . . ; relate the strategy to a written method. Understand that in adding or subtracting three-digit numbers, one adds or subtracts hundreds and hundreds, tens and tens, ones and ones; and sometimes it is necessary to compose or decompose tens or hundreds. **Also 2.NBT.2.9**
MAFS.K12.MP.2.1, MP.3.1, MP.7.1

$$243 + 354 = \underline{\hspace{2cm}}$$

Find 238 + 126.

Hundreds	Tens	Ones
2 hundreds	3 tens	8 ones
1 hundred	2 tens	6 ones

You can show each addend with place-value blocks.

Join the hundreds, the tens, and the ones. Regroup if you can.

Hundreds	Tens	Ones
3 hundreds	5 tens	14 ones or 1 ten and 4 ones
3 hundreds 300	6 tens 60	4 ones 4

You can regroup 10 ones as 1 ten.

So, 238 + 126 = 364.

Convince Me! Are the tens regrouped in the example above? How do you know?

☆ **Guided Practice** ☆ Use place-value blocks to find each sum. Regroup if needed.

1. 223 + 106 = _____

Hundreds	Tens	Ones

2. 149 + 362 = _____

Hundreds	Tens	Ones

Topic 10 | Lesson 3

Name _____

Independent Practice ☆ Use and draw blocks to find each sum. Regroup if needed.

3. 151 + 324 = _____

Hundreds	Tens	Ones

4. 250 + 298 = _____

Hundreds	Tens	Ones

5. 258 + 109 = _____

Hundreds	Tens	Ones

6. 187 + 246 = _____

Hundreds	Tens	Ones

7. 236 + 318 = _____

Hundreds	Tens	Ones

8. 432 + 365 = _____

Hundreds	Tens	Ones

9. **Number Sense** Jamal says that the sum of 183 + 198 is less than 300. Is Jamal's answer reasonable? Why or why not?

Both addends are close to 200.

_____

_____

_____

10. **Reasoning** 156 children in a school are girls.
148 children in that school are boys.
How many children go to that school?

How do numbers in the problem relate to each other?

_____ children

11. **Higher Order Thinking** Write an addition problem about stickers. Use 3-digit numbers. Then solve the problem.

_____

_____

_____

12. 🌀 **Assessment Practice** Which is the sum of 129 + 268? 🏁 2.NBT.2.7

Hundreds	Tens	Ones

Ⓐ 292

Ⓑ 294

Ⓒ 389

Ⓓ 397

Regroup if needed.

© Pearson Education, Inc. 2

Solve & Share

Oak School has 256 students. Pine School has 371 students. How many students do the schools have in all?
Use place-value blocks to help. Draw your blocks below and solve.

I can ...
use models and place value to add 3-digit numbers.

MAFS.2.NBT.2.7 Add and subtract within 1000, using concrete models or drawings and strategies . . . ; relate the strategy to a written method. Understand that in adding or subtracting three-digit numbers, one adds or subtracts hundreds and hundreds, tens and tens, ones and ones; and sometimes it is necessary to compose or decompose tens or hundreds. **Also 2.NBT.2.9**
MAFS.K12.MP.3.1, MP.4.1, MP.6.1

Hundreds	Tens	Ones

Find 372 + 145.
Draw place-value blocks.

Hundreds	Tens	Ones
3 hundreds	7 tens	2 ones
1 hundred	4 tens	5 ones

Join the the hundreds, the tens, and the ones.

Hundreds	Tens	Ones
4 hundreds	11 tens	7 ones
400	110	7

The partial sums are 400, 110, and 7.

Add the partial sums to get the final sum.

```
  400
  110
+   7
-----
  517
```

So, 372 + 145 = 517.

Convince Me! Look at the example above. Why don't the 11 tens need to be regrouped to get the final sum?

☆ **Guided Practice** ☆   Draw blocks to find the partial sums. Record the partial sums to find the sum.

1. 236 + 252 = _____

Hundreds	Tens	Ones

```
  400
   80
+   8
-----
  488
```

2. 328 + 124 = _____

Hundreds	Tens	Ones

Independent Practice

Draw blocks to find the partial sums.
Record the partial sums to find the sum.

3. 372 + 281 = _____

Hundreds	Tens	Ones

4. 429 + 163 = _____

Hundreds	Tens	Ones

5. 174 + 245 = _____

Hundreds	Tens	Ones

6. Higher Order Thinking Ben said that the sum of
157 and 137 is 284. Nikki said that Ben made a
mistake. Who is correct? Explain.

Add 157 and 137.
Do you get the same
sum as Ben?

_____

_____

Solve each problem below. You can use models to help.

You can draw blocks to model the problem. Use partial sums to solve.

7. **Model** On Friday, 354 people went to the fair. On Saturday, 551 people went to the fair.

How many people went to the fair in all?

Hundreds	Tens	Ones

_____ people

8. **Higher Order Thinking** Write an addition problem in which the partial sum for tens is greater than 10 tens. Draw blocks and show partial sums to solve.

_____ + _____ = _____

Hundreds	Tens	Ones

9. **Assessment Practice** Find 448 + 323. Draw place-value blocks and show partial sums to solve. 2.NBT.2.7

448 + 323 = _____

Hundreds	Tens	Ones

Name _____

Activity

Solve & Share

On Monday, 248 people visit the museum.

On Tuesday, 325 people visit the museum.

How many people visit the museum on Monday and Tuesday?

Solve any way you choose. Be prepared to explain your thinking.

I can ...
add 3-digit numbers using place value and partial sums.

MAFS.2.NBT.2.7 Add and subtract within 1000, using concrete models or drawings and strategies . . . ; relate the strategy to a written method. Understand that in adding or subtracting three-digit numbers, one adds or subtracts hundreds and hundreds, tens and tens, ones and ones; and sometimes it is necessary to compose or decompose tens or hundreds. **Also 2.NBT.2.9**
MAFS.K12.MP.3.1, MP.7.1

_____ people

Find 257 + 384.
You can draw blocks to show the addends.

Hundreds	Tens	Ones
(blocks)	(blocks)	(blocks)

Add the partial sums to find the sum.

	Hundreds	Tens	Ones
	2	5	7
+	3	8	4
Hundreds:	5	0	0
Tens:	1	3	0
Ones:		1	1
Sum =	6	4	1

Here is how you can write the addition.

```
  2 5 7
+ 3 8 4
-------
  5 0 0
  1 3 0
+   1 1
-------
  6 4 1
```

So, 257 + 384 = 641.

Convince Me! Can the problem above be solved by adding the ones first, then the tens, and then the hundreds? Explain.

☆ **Guided Practice** ☆ Add. Use partial sums. Show your work. Use place-value blocks if needed.

1. 425 + 148 = _____

	Hundreds	Tens	Ones
	4	2	5
+	1	4	8
Hundreds:	5	0	0
Tens:		6	0
Ones:		1	3
Sum =			

2. 394 + 276 = _____

```
  3 9 4
+ 2 7 6
```

Keep place values in line when you write each partial sum.

© Pearson Education, Inc. 2

Name _____

Independent Practice ✰   Add. Use partial sums. Show your work.

3.   347
   +242

4.   183
   +249

5.   278
   +406

6.   367
   +493

7.   518
   +347

8. **Higher Order Thinking** Mark found the sum of 127 and 345. Explain his mistake. What is the correct sum?

Mark's Work: 127
                  + 345
   Hundreds: 400
   Tens: 6
   Ones: +   12
                  418

_____

_____

_____

9. **Reasoning** Rhea has a $100 bill, four $20 bills, one $10 bill, and three $5 bills. Is this amount greater or less than $210? Explain.

_____

_____

_____

_____

10. Look for Patterns 349 people are on a boat. 255 people are on another boat. How many people are on both boats?

You can use place value and partial sums to add.

_____ people

11. 163 students are in first grade. 217 students are in second grade. How many students are in both grades?

_____ students

12. Higher Order Thinking Choose a number between 100 and 400. Add 384 to your number. What is the sum? Show your work.

Explain the steps you took to find the sum.

_____

_____

_____

13. ⬤ **Assessment Practice** Which is the same amount as 238 + 164? Choose all that apply. 🔵 2.NBT.2.7

☐ 200 + 190 + 12   ☐ 300 + 90 + 12   ☐ 402   ☐ 400 + 10 + 2

     Topic 10 | Lesson 5

Name _____

Solve & Share

Find 375 + 235. Explain your strategy. Then explain why your strategy works.

I can ...
use different addition strategies to add and explain why the strategies work.

MAFS.2.NBT.2.9 Explain why addition and subtraction strategies work, using place value and the properties of operations. **Also** 2.NBT.2.7
MAFS.K12.MP.2.1, MP.3.1, MP.4.1

Lauren, Nate, and Josh use different ways to find 257 + 126.

Lauren uses an open number line. She starts at 257 and mentally adds up the hundreds, the tens, and the ones.

Lauren's Number Line

Nate draws place-value blocks. He regroups 10 ones as 1 ten.

Nate's Place-Value Blocks

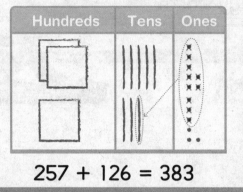

257 + 126 = 383

Josh uses place value. He adds the ones, the tens, and then hundreds.

Josh's Partial Sums

```
  257
+ 126
   13
   70
+ 300
  383
```

Why does each strategy work?

Convince Me! Choose a strategy shown above. Explain why it works.

⭐ **Guided Practice** ⭐ Use the strategy to solve the problem. Show your work. Then explain your work.

1. 624 + 248 = 872

Start at 624. Add 2 hundreds. Then add 4 tens. Count on 6 to get to 870, then add 2 more to reach 872. The jumps add up to 248.

Tools   Assessment

Independent Practice

Choose any strategy to solve each addition problem. Show your work. Then explain why the strategy works.

2. $212 + 487 =$ _____

_____

_____

3. $874 + 109 =$ _____

_____

_____

4. $419 + 532 =$ _____

5. $650 + 270 =$ _____

How many different ways can you use?

_____

_____

6. **Reasoning** Lee School needs 407 folders for its students. Jefferson School needs 321 folders for its students. How many folders do both schools need?

_____ folders

7. **Reasoning** There are 229 people at the football game. 108 more people arrive at the game. How many people are at the football game now?

_____ people

8. **Higher Order Thinking** Tommy found $125 + 598$. Since 598 is close to 600, he added $125 + 600 = 725$. Then he subtracted 2 to get 723.

Why did Tommy subtract 2? Explain.

9. **Assessment Practice** There are 192 ants on an ant farm. 397 more ants join the ant farm. How many ants are on the ant farm now? Use the number line to solve. Explain. 2.NBT.2.9

Name _____

Solve & Share

Solve these problems any way you choose. Explain patterns you see.

$63 + 28 = ?$

$263 + 128 = ?$

I can ...
solve problems and explain patterns I see.

MAFS.K12.MP.8.1 Look for and express regularity in repeated reasoning.
Also MP.1.1, MP.2.1, MP.4.1
MAFS.2.NBT.2.7 Add and subtract within 1000, using concrete models or drawings and strategies . . . ; relate the strategy to a written method. Understand that in adding or subtracting three-digit numbers, one adds or subtracts hundreds and hundreds, tens and tens, ones and ones; and sometimes it is necessary to compose or decompose tens or hundreds. **Also 2.NBT.2.9**

$63 + 28 = ?$	$263 + 128 = ?$

Thinking Habits

What can I use from one problem to help with another problem?

Are there things that repeat?

How is adding 3-digit numbers like adding 2-digit numbers?

$24 + 36 = ?$

$324 + 136 = ?$

I can use what I know and look for things that repeat. I can check my work as I add each place.

Use two open number lines.

Use partial sums.

```
   24        324
 + 36      + 136
   10         10
 + 50         50
   60       + 400
              460
```

$24 + 36 = 60$

$324 + 136 = 460$

I used repeated reasoning. I added the same ones to ones and tens to tens in both problems. I repeated this with two different strategies.

Convince Me! If you start with 36 and add on 24, in the example above, will you get the same sum? Explain.

☆ **Guided Practice** ☆

Use repeated reasoning to solve the two problems. Circle the digits that are the same in the sums. Explain why the sums are different.

1. $57 + 29 = $ ____

```
   57
 + 29
   16
 + 70
```

$157 + 229 = $ ____

© Pearson Education, Inc. 2

Topic 10 | Lesson 7

Tools Assessment

Independent Practice ☆ Solve each problem.

2. Write a problem where you need to regroup to make a ten or a hundred. Each addend must be three digits. Draw place-value blocks to solve your problem. Then explain why you needed to regroup.

_____ + _____ = _____

Hundreds	Tens	Ones

_____

_____

_____

3. Write a problem where you do not need to regroup to make a ten or a hundred. Each addend must be three digits. Draw place-value blocks to solve your problem. Then explain why you did not need to regroup.

_____ + _____ = _____

Hundreds	Tens	Ones

_____

_____

_____

Problem Solving

Tickets Sold

The table shows how many tickets were sold at a theater.

How many tickets were sold on Thursday and Saturday in all?

TICKETS

25145843

Tickets Sold	
Thursday	128
Friday	245
Saturday	367

25145843

4. Make Sense Which numbers and operation can you use to solve the problem? MP.1.1

_____

_____

_____

5. Model Write an equation that shows the problem you need to solve. MP.4.1

_____ ◯ _____ = _____

6. Generalize Use what you know about adding 3-digit numbers to solve the problem. Explain what you did. 2.NBT.2.7, 2.NBT.2.9, MP.8.1

_____

_____

_____

© Pearson Education, Inc. 2

Name _____

Point & Tally

Find a partner. Get paper and a pencil. Each partner chooses a different color: light blue or dark blue.

Partner 1 and Partner 2 each point to a black number at the same time. Both partners subtract Partner 2's number from Partner 1's number.

If the answer is on your color, you get a tally mark. Work until one partner gets seven tally marks.

I can ...
subtract within 100.

 MAFS.2.NBT.2.5

Partner 1							Partner 2
59	53	19	43	62	37	30	**45**
78	48	65	81	32	51	76	**27**
92	14	71	58	66	48	25	**16**
82	44	37	55	47	33	67	**11**
64							**34**

Tally Marks for Partner 1

Tally Marks for Partner 2

A-Z Glossary

Word List
- addend
- break apart
- digits
- hundreds
- mental math
- open number line
- partial sum
- sum

Understand Vocabulary

Choose a term from the Word List to complete each sentence.

1. When adding $193 + 564$, the sum of $90 + 60$ is called a

   _____.

2. In $709 + 187$, 709 is an _____.

3. You can use an _____ to count on.

4. In 841, there are

   _____ hundreds.

5. Give the value of each digit in 610.

   _____

6. Use mental math to find $198 + 362$.

   _____

Use Vocabulary in Writing

7. Use words to tell how to find $249 + 201$. Use terms from the Word List.

   _____
   _____
   _____
   _____
   _____

Name _____

Set A

You can use mental math to add 10 or 100 to 362.

$362 + 10 = 372$

Add 1 ten

$362 + 100 = 462$

Add 1 hundred

Add using place-value blocks or mental math.

1. $600 + 10 =$ _____

2. $345 + 100 =$ _____

3. $543 + 100 =$ _____

4. $800 + 100 =$ _____

5. $799 + 10 =$ _____

6. $119 + 10 =$ _____

Set B

You can use an open number line to add. Find $327 + 126$.

First, place 327 on the line and then count on by 100s, 10s, and 1s.

$$+100 \quad +10 \quad +10 \quad +6$$

327   427   437   447 453

So, $327 + 126 =$ 453.

Use an open number line to find each sum.

7. $594 + 132 =$ _____

8. $157 + 245 =$ _____

You can draw place-value blocks and use partial sums to add.
Find $276 + 137$.

Hundreds	Tens	Ones
2	7	6
+ 1	3	7

	Hundreds	Tens	Ones
Hundreds:	3	0	0
Tens:	1	0	0
Ones:		1	3
Sum =	4	1	3

Add. Use partial sums. Show your work.
Use drawings of blocks if needed.

9. $408 + 326 =$ _____

Hundreds	Tens	Ones
4	0	8
+ 3	2	6

	Hundreds	Tens	Ones
Hundreds:			
Tens:			
Ones:			
Sum =			

Thinking Habits

Repeated Reasoning

What can I use from one problem to help with another problem?

Are there things that repeat?

Solve each problem. Use partial sums and repeated reasoning. Use drawings of blocks if needed.

10.

```
   68          168
 + 14        + 214
```

Circle the digits that are alike in each sum.

1. Emily has 100 sun stickers. She has 382 star stickers and 10 moon stickers. How many sun and star stickers does Emily have?

Ⓐ 492   Ⓒ 393

Ⓑ 482   Ⓓ 392

2. Tyrone collects baseball cards. He gives 138 cards to his friend. Now he has 428 cards. How many cards did Tyrone have before he gave some away?

_____ cards

3. Use the open number line to solve the problem. Write the missing numbers in the boxes.

$421 + 250 = ?$

$421 + 250 =$ _____

4. Which is the same amount as $528 + 167$? Choose all that apply.

☐ $500 + 80 + 15$ ☐ $500 + 180 + 15$ ☐ $600 + 90 + 5$ ☐ $600 + 80 + 15$

5. Choose all the equations in which the sum is 488.

☐ $478 + 10 = ?$ ☐ $388 + 100 = ?$ ☐ $248 + 240 = ?$ ☐ $200 + 265 = ?$

6. Rich has 335 pennies.

Beth has 58 more pennies than Rich.

How many pennies do they have in all?

Ⓐ 277

Ⓑ 393

Ⓒ 628

Ⓓ 728

Hundreds	Tens	Ones

7. Use place value and partial sums to find 472 + 256. Show your work.

	Hundreds	Tens	Ones
	4	7	2
+	2	5	6
Hundreds:			
Tens:			
Ones:			
Sum:			

472 + 256 = _____

8. Molly reads 184 pages. Pat reads 294 pages. What is the total number of pages they read in all?

Use any strategy. Show your work and explain.

_____ pages

9. On Saturday, 449 people visit the zoo. On Sunday, 423 people visit the zoo. How many people visit the zoo in all?

Use the open number line to solve. Explain your work.

Name _____

Recycling Race
Westbrook School is having a recycling contest. The table shows the number of cans each grade collected in February.

Cans Collected in February	
First Grade	264
Second Grade	302
Third Grade	392
Fourth Grade	425

1. How many cans did the first-grade students and the second-grade students collect in all?
Use the open number line to solve.

2.NBT.2.7, MP.4.1, MP.5.1

_____ cans

2. Bruce used partial sums to find how many cans the third-grade students and fourth-grade students collected in all. 2.NBT.2.7, 2.NBT.2.9, MP.1.1, MP.3.1

$$
\begin{array}{r}
392 \\
+\ 425 \\
\end{array}
$$

Hundreds: 700
Tens: 11
Ones: + 7
718

Do you agree with his answer?
Circle **yes** or **no**.

Explain your answer.

_____
_____
_____
_____
_____

3. Which two grades collected a total of 689 cans? Choose any strategy to solve the problem. Show your work. Explain which strategy you used.

2.NBT.2.7, 2.NBT.2.9, MP.3.1

[ ]

The _____ grade and the _____ grade collected a total of 689 cans.

Here are some addition strategies you have learned.

Addition Strategies

Open Number Line   Partial Sums
Compensation   Place-Value Blocks
Mental Math   Regrouping
Break Apart Numbers

4. The second-grade collected 432 cans in March. They collected 198 cans in April. Tom and Bill find how many cans the class collected in March and April. 2.NBT.2.7, 2.NBT.2.9, MP.1.1, MP.3.1

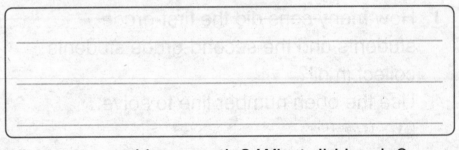

Tom's Way	Bill's Way
432	432
+ 198	+ 198
10	10
120	12
+ 500	+ 500
630	522

Who added correctly? Explain.

_____
_____
_____

Who answered incorrectly? What did he do?

_____
_____
_____

© Pearson Education, Inc. 2

Topic 10 | Performance Task

Subtract Within 1,000 Using Models and Strategies

Essential Question: What are strategies for subtracting numbers to 1,000?

Bees help move pollen from one flower to another!

Moving the pollen helps plants grow fruit and vegetables.

MAFS.2.NBT.2.7, 2.NBT.2.8, 2.NBT.2.9, 2.MD.3.8
MAFS.K12.MP.1.1, MP.2.1, MP.3.1, MP.4.1, MP.5.1, MP.6.1, MP.7.1, MP.8.1

Wow! Let's do this project and learn more.

enVision STEM Project: Making Models

Find Out Use a paintbrush as a model of a bee's leg. Dip the brush in a bowl of sugar. Then dip the brush in a bowl of pepper. Take turns. What happens to the sugar? What happens to the pepper?

Journal: Make a Book Show what you learn in a book. In your book, also:

• Tell how bees help move pollen between plants.

• Show how to use a model to help subtract three-digit numbers.

Name _____

Review What You Know

Vocabulary

1. Circle each number that is **less than** 607.

   598

   608

   706

2. Circle each number that is **greater than** 299.

   352

   300

   298

3. Circle the group of numbers that **decrease** by 100 from left to right.

   650, 550, 450, 350

   320, 420, 520, 620

   570, 560, 550, 540

Subtraction Facts

4. Write each difference.

   $14 - 7 =$ _____

   $11 - 4 =$ _____

   $16 - 9 =$ _____

   Think of addition facts to help.

Partial Differences

5. Use partial differences to find $54 - 29$.

Math Story

6. Ben has 64 comic books. He gives 36 comic books to friends. How many comic books does Ben have left?

   _____ comic books

Name _____

PROJECT 11A

How tall is the world's tallest redwood tree?

Project: Create a Redwood Trees Booklet

PROJECT 11B

Where does a lot of snow fall?

Project: Build a Snow Sculpture

PROJECT 11C

How high are Florida's mountains?

Project: Make a Poster About Florida Mountains

Math Modeling

The Chemistry Set

Video

Before watching the video, talk to a classmate:

When was the last time you mixed something together? What happened to the items you mixed? How did they change?

MAFS.K12.MP.4.1 Model with mathematics. **Also MP.1.1, MP.5.1**
MAFS.2.NBT.2.7 Add and subtract within 1000, using concrete models or drawings and strategies based on place value, properties of operations, and/or the relationship between addition and subtraction; relate the strategy to a written method. Understand that in adding or subtracting three digit numbers, one adds or subtracts hundreds and hundreds, tens and tens, ones and ones; and sometimes it is necessary to compose or decompose tens or hundreds.
Also 2.NBT.2.9

© Pearson Education, Inc. 2

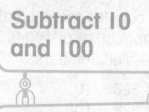

Solve & Share

Jill's Pumpkin Patch sells straw men.

A large straw man costs $134.

A medium straw man costs $10 less than a large straw man.

A small straw man costs $100 less than a large straw man.

What is the cost of a medium straw man? A small straw man?

Use dollar bills, place-value blocks, or mental math to solve.

Be ready to explain how you solved the problem.

I can ...

subtract 10 or 100 mentally using what I know about place value.

MAFS.2.NBT.2.8 Mentally add 10 or 100 to a given number 100–900, and mentally subtract 10 or 100 from a given number 100–900. Also 2.NBT.2.9, 2.MD.3.8.c MAFS.K12.MP.3.1, MP.4.1, MP.7.1

You can use mental math to subtract 10 or 100 from three-digit numbers.

Find 328 − 10.
Find 328 − 100.

328

Place value can help me subtract mentally.

328 − 10 = _____

2 tens minus 1 ten equals 1 ten.

So, 328 − 10 = 318 .

328 − 100 = _____

3 hundreds minus 1 hundred equals 2 hundreds.

So, 328 − 100 = 228 .

Sometimes subtracting 10 changes the tens and hundreds digits.
Find 500 − 10.

I know 500 = 50 tens. 50 tens minus 1 ten equals 49 tens or 490.

So, 500 − 10 = 490 .

Convince Me! Use mental math to find 457 − 10 and 457 − 100. Explain your reasoning.

Guided Practice

Subtract. Use place-value blocks or mental math. Then write an equation to show the subtraction.

1.

214 − 10 = 204

2.

_____ − _____ = _____

3.

_____ − _____ = _____

4.

_____ − _____ = _____

© Pearson Education, Inc. 2

Topic 11 | Lesson 1

Tools Assessment

Independent Practice ☆ Subtract. Use place-value blocks or mental math.

5. $250 - 10 =$ _____

6. $604 - 10 =$ _____

7. $\$102 - \$100 =$ _____

8. $719 - 10 =$ _____

9. $\$400 - \$100 =$ _____

10. $308 - 10 =$ _____

11. $520 - 100 =$ _____

12. $975 - 10 =$ _____

13. $143 - 100 =$ _____

14. $\$825 - \$10 =$ _____

15. $409 - 10 =$ _____

16. $\$200 - \$100 =$ _____

Algebra Find the missing numbers. Use mental math to solve.

17. $362 - \boxed{} = 352$

18. $801 - \boxed{} = 701$

19. $449 = 549 - \boxed{}$

20. $657 - \boxed{} = 647$

21. $215 - \boxed{} = 205$

22. $700 - \boxed{} = 690$

23. **enVision®** STEM Marni is studying facts about bees. She finds that one type of bee can pollinate 955 plants each day. A different type of bee pollinates 100 fewer plants. How many plants does it pollinate?

_____ plants

24. **Model** Alex has five $100 bills, three $10 bills, and four $1 bills. He buys a pair of shoes for $100. How much money does he have left?

_____

25. **Higher Order Thinking** Think of a 3-digit number. Write a story about subtracting 100 from your number. Then complete the equation to show your subtraction.

_____ _ _____ = _____

26. 🄰 **Assessment Practice** Which equations are true? Choose all that apply. 🄣 2.NBT.2.8

☐ 303 − 10 = 293

☐ 493 − 100 = 393

☐ 563 − 10 = 453

☐ 309 − 100 = 299

Activity

☆ Solve & Share ☆

There are 224 girls and some boys in a parade. There are 471 children in the parade. How many boys are in the parade?

Use the open number line to solve the problem. Show your work.

Lesson 11-2

Subtract on an Open Number Line

I can ...
use an open number line to add up to subtract 3-digit numbers.

MAFS.2.NBT.2.7 Add and subtract within 1000, using concrete models or drawings and strategies. . . ; relate the strategy to a written method. Understand that in adding or subtracting three-digit numbers, one adds or subtracts hundreds and hundreds, tens and tens, ones and ones; and sometimes it is necessary to compose or decompose tens or hundreds. **Also 2.NBT.2.9** MAFS.K12.MP.2.1, MP.4.1, MP.6.1

←————————————————————→

Find 382 − 247. Use an open number line.

One Way You can add up to find the difference.

+100
+10 +10 +10 +3 +2

247   347   367 382
       357   377
            380

100 + 10 + 10 + 10 + 3 + 2 = 135

Add up from 247, the number you are subtracting. Stop at 382.

Another Way You can count back to find the difference.

+3 −50   −100   −100

132 135   182   282   382

So, 382 − 247 = 135.

You can check your work by adding.

247 + 135 = 382.
So, 135 is correct.

247 is close to 250. You can count back 250 and then add 3 to subtract 247.

Convince Me! What is another way you could add up to find 382 − 247? Explain.

★ **Guided Practice**   Use the open number line to subtract.

1. 573 − 459 = _____

+100   +10 +1+1+1+1

459   559   569 | 571 | 573
                           570   572

2. 672 − 547 = _____

© Pearson Education, Inc. 2

Name _____

Independent Practice ☆   Use the open number line to subtract.

3. 530 − 318 = _____

4. 735 − 429 = _____

5. 802 − 688 = _____

6. (A-Z) **Vocabulary** Complete the sentences using each word below once.

ones   **add**   **number**

You can add up to subtract on an open number line.

Start at the _____ you are subtracting.

_____ up hundreds, tens, and

_____.

Stop at the number you subtract from.

7. Reasoning Yun has 780 blocks. Marsha has 545 fewer blocks than Yun. How many blocks does Marsha have?

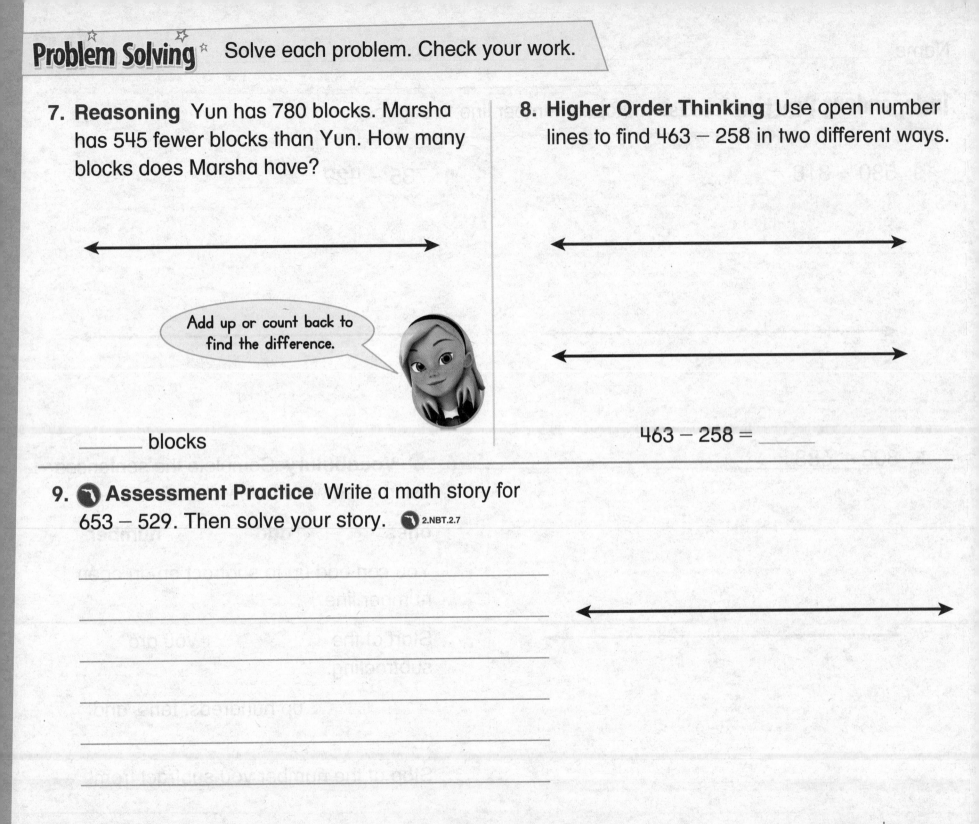

Add up or count back to find the difference.

_____ blocks

8. Higher Order Thinking Use open number lines to find 463 − 258 in two different ways.

463 − 258 = _____

9. 🏵 **Assessment Practice** Write a math story for 653 − 529. Then solve your story. 🏵 **2.NBT.2.7**

_____

_____

_____

_____

_____

Activity

Solve & Share

Use place-value blocks to find 482 − 127. Tell which place value you subtracted first and why. Then draw a picture to show your work.

I can ...
use models to subtract 3-digit numbers.

MAFS.2.NBT.2.7 Add and subtract within 1000, using concrete models or drawings and strategies . . . ; relate the strategy to a written method. Understand that in adding or subtracting three-digit numbers, one adds or subtracts hundreds and hundreds, tens and tens, ones and ones; and sometimes it is necessary to compose or decompose tens or hundreds. **Also 2.NBT.2.9**
MAFS.K12.MP.1.1, MP.4.1, MP.5.1

Find 335 − 117.
Show 335 using hundreds, tens, and ones.

Hundreds	Tens	Ones
3 hundreds	3 tens	5 ones

You can start by taking away hundreds and tens.

Take away 1 hundred and 1 ten.

Hundreds	Tens	Ones
2 hundreds	2 tens	5 ones

Take away 7 ones.
First take away 5 ones.
Regroup 1 ten as 10 ones.
Then take away 2 ones.

Hundreds	Tens	Ones
2 hundreds	1 ten	8 ones

So,
335 − 117 = 218.

Convince Me! Explain why regrouping works in the problem above.

✰ **Guided Practice** ✰ Use and draw blocks to find each difference. Show your work.

1. 326 − 143 = 183

Hundreds	Tens	Ones

2. 363 − 127 = _____

Hundreds	Tens	Ones

3. 546 − 271 = _____

Hundreds	Tens	Ones

© Pearson Education, Inc. 2

Name _____

Independent Practice

Use and draw blocks to find each difference. Show your work.

4. 314 − 152 = _____

Hundreds	Tens	Ones

5. 653 − 419 = _____

Hundreds	Tens	Ones

6. 438 − 162 = _____

Hundreds	Tens	Ones

7. 662 − 480 = _____

Hundreds	Tens	Ones

8. 999 − 834 = _____

9. 599 − 209 = _____

10. 954 − 738 = _____

11. Number Sense Tyler says that the difference of 676 − 367 is greater than 200. Is what Tyler says reasonable? Why or why not?

_____

_____

_____

Sometimes it can help to use numbers that are close but easier to subtract.

Solve each problem below.
Show your work.

12. Tia collected cans to raise money for school. She collected 569 cans on Monday. Tia collected some more cans on Tuesday. Now she has 789 cans. How many cans did Tia collect on Tuesday?

_____ cans

13. Make Sense Josh has these bills. How much money does he have?

_____

14. Higher Order Thinking Write a subtraction problem about recycling. Use 3-digit numbers. Then solve the problem.

15. 🦉 **Assessment Practice** Use the place-value-blocks to find 864 − 319. Which is the difference? 🦉 **2.NBT.2.7**

Ⓐ 454

Ⓑ 535

Regroup if needed.

Ⓒ 545

Ⓓ 555

Solve & Share

Larissa has $353. She buys a pair of basketball shoes for $117. How much money does she have left over?

Use or draw place-value blocks to solve. Be ready to explain what you did and why it works.

I can ...
use models and place value to subtract.

MAFS.2.NBT.2.7 Add and subtract within 1000, using concrete models or drawings and strategies . . . ; relate the strategy to a written method. Understand that in adding or subtracting three-digit numbers, one adds or subtracts hundreds and hundreds, tens and tens, ones and ones; and sometimes it is necessary to compose or decompose tens or hundreds. Also 2.NBT.2.9, 2.MD.3.8 MAFS.K12.MP.1.1, MP.2.1, MP.4.1

Find 328 − 133.

One Way
Subtract 1 hundred from 3 hundreds.

"I can record partial differences."

```
 328
−100
 228
```

Hundreds	Tens	Ones
□ □ ⊠	‖	⋮ :

2 hundreds   2 tens   8 ones

Subtract 3 tens.
First, subtract 2 tens.
Regroup 1 hundred as 10 tens.
Then subtract 1 ten.

```
 328
−100
 228
− 20
 208
− 10
 198
```

Hundreds	Tens	Ones
□ (□)	‖‖‖ ✕✕	⋮ :

1 hundred   9 tens   8 ones

Subtract 3 ones from 8 ones.

```
 328
−100
 228
− 20
 208
− 10
 198
−  3
 195
```

Hundreds	Tens	Ones
□	‖‖‖‖‖	⋮ ✕✕✕

1 hundred   9 tens   5 ones

So, 328 − 133 = 195.

Convince Me! Find 254 − 174. Jason says he can subtract 100, and then 4, and then 70 to find the difference. Do you agree? Explain.

Guided Practice Draw blocks to find the partial differences. Record the partial differences to find the difference.

1. 485 − 136 = 349

```
 485
−  5    Subtract 5 ones.
 480
−  1    Subtract 1 one.
 479
− 30    Subtract 3 tens.
 449
−100    Subtract 1 hundred.
 349
```

Hundreds	Tens	Ones
□ □ □ ⊠	✕✕✕ ‖‖‖‖‖0	⋮ :✕✕✕✕

Tools   Assessment

Independent Practice Draw blocks to find the partial differences. Record the partial differences to find the difference.

2. 598 − 319 = _____

Hundreds	Tens	Ones

3. 794 − 452 = _____

Hundreds	Tens	Ones

4. 871 − 355 = _____

Hundreds	Tens	Ones

Solve. Draw blocks to help.

5. Higher Order Thinking There were 642 people at the beach. There were 271 adults at the beach. The rest were children. How many children were at the beach?

Hundreds	Tens	Ones

_____ children

Solve each problem. You can use models to help. Show your work.

6. **Model** Jeff has 517 baseball cards. He has 263 football cards. How many more baseball cards than football cards does he have?

Can you use drawings of place-value blocks to show partial differences?

Hundreds	Tens	Ones

_____ more baseball cards

7. **Reasoning** Felipe has 453 stamps in his collection. Emily has 762 stamps in her collection. How many more stamps does Emily have?

Hundreds	Tens	Ones

_____ more stamps

8. 🌀 **Assessment Practice** Which numbers complete this partial difference problem for $423 - 219$? Choose all that apply. 🌀 2.NBT.2.7

$$
\begin{array}{r}
423 \\
-\ 10 \\
\hline
413 \\
-\ 200 \\
\hline
? \\
-\ 3 \\
\hline
210 \\
-\ 6 \\
\hline
?
\end{array}
$$

☐ 213   ☐ 204

☐ 210   ☐ 200

Name _____

Solve & Share

Find 532 − 215. Use any strategy. Then explain why your strategy works.

I can ...
explain why subtraction strategies work using models, place value, and mental math.

MAFS.2.NBT.2.9 Explain why addition and subtraction strategies work, using place value and the properties of operations.
Also 2.NBT.2.7
MAFS.K12.MP.2.1, MP.3.1, MP.4.1

Find 437 − 245. Use any strategy.

One Way Draw place-value blocks to show 437. Regroup 1 hundred as 10 tens. Then subtract.

So, 437 − 245 = ___192___ .

Another Way Use an open number line to subtract.

So, 437 − 245 = ___192___ .

You can record partial differences.

```
 437
−200
 237
− 30
 207
− 10
 197
−  5
 192
```

Convince Me! Show how to count up on the open number line to find 437 − 245. Explain why your way works.

⭐ **Guided Practice** ⭐ Subtract any way you choose. Show your work. Then explain why the strategy works.

1. 345 − 116 = __229__

© Pearson Education, Inc. 2

Topic 11 | Lesson 5

Tools Assessment

Independent Practice

Choose any strategy to solve each subtraction problem. Show your work. Then explain why the strategy works.

2. $312 - 179 =$ _____

_____

_____

_____

3. $464 - 155 =$ _____

_____

_____

_____

4. $612 - 478 =$ _____

_____

_____

_____

5. **Number Sense** Use place value to find $748 - 319$. Complete the equations.

$$319 = 300 + \underline{\quad} + 9$$

Hundreds: $748 - \underline{\quad} = \underline{\quad}$

Tens: $\underline{\quad} - 10 = \underline{\quad}$

Ones: $\underline{\quad} - \underline{\quad} = \underline{\quad}$

6. **Explain** Ava wants to use mental math to find 352 − 149. Show how she could find the difference. Is this a good strategy for Ava to use? Explain why or why not.

7. **Higher Order Thinking** Kristin found 562 − 399 = 163 using an open number line. She added up to subtract. First she added 1, then 100, and then 62.

Draw Kristin's number line. Do you think Kristin's strategy was helpful? Explain.

8. 🅐 **Assessment Practice** Joff counted back on this open number line to find 812 − 125.

Use the numbers on the cards to find the missing numbers in the open number line. Write the missing numbers. 🅐 2.NBT.2.9

| 702 | 812 | 687 | 712 |

692

© Pearson Education, Inc. 2

Name _____

Solve & Share

Jody wants to bake 350 muffins.
She bakes one batch of 160 muffins and one batch of 145 muffins. How many more muffins does Jody need to bake?

Solve any way you choose. Show your work.
Be prepared to explain why your way works.

I can ...
solve problems that take more than one step.

MAFS.K12.MP.1.1 Make sense of problems and persevere in solving them.
Also MP.2.1, MP.3.1, MP.8.1
MAFS.2.NBT.2.7 Add and subtract within 1000, using concrete models or drawings and strategies. . . ; relate the strategy to a written method. Understand that in adding or subtracting three-digit numbers, one adds or subtracts hundreds and hundreds, tens and tens, ones and ones; and sometimes it is necessary to compose or decompose tens or hundreds. **Also 2.NBT.2.9**

Thinking Habits
What do I know?

What do I need to find?

How can I check that my solution makes sense?

Grade 2 wants to sell 10 more tickets to the school play than Grade 1.

Grade 1 sold 476 tickets. Grade 2 sold 439 tickets.

How many more tickets does Grade 2 have to sell to reach their goal?

How can I make sense of the problem?

I can see what I know. I can find hidden questions. I can choose a strategy to solve the problem.

An easy first step is to answer the hidden question.

What is the Grade 2 goal?

Grade 2 Goal

476 + 10 = 486 tickets

Now I can subtract the number of tickets Grade 2 sold from their goal.

486 − 439 = ?

Count up to subtract.
439 + 1 = 440
440 + 46 = 486
486 − 439 = 47

Grade 2 needs to sell 47 more tickets.

Convince Me! What questions can you ask yourself when you get stuck? Be ready to explain how questions can help.

☆ **Guided Practice** ☆ Solve the problem. Remember to ask yourself questions to help. Show your work.

1. Kim had 455 shells. First, she gives 134 of the shells to a friend. Then she finds 54 more shells. How many shells does Kim have now?

What will you find first? Which operation will you use?

© Pearson Education, Inc. 2

Name _____

Independent Practice ☆ Use the table to solve each problem. Show your work.

Weights of Wild Animals (in pounds)				
Animal	Arctic Wolf	Black Bear	Grizzly Bear	Mule Deer	Polar Bear
Weight	176	270	990	198	945

2. How much heavier is a grizzly bear than an arctic wolf and a black bear together?

3. How much less does a black bear weigh than the weight of 2 mule deer?

4. How much more does a polar bear weigh than an arctic wolf, a black bear, and a mule deer together?

You know how to add three 2-digit numbers.

How can that help you add three 3-digit numbers?

Problem Solving

Big Truck

The picture at the right shows the height of a truck and the height of a smokestack on top of the truck. The height of a bridge is 144 inches.

Use the information at the right.
Can the truck travel under the bridge?

27 inches

112 inches

5. **Make Sense** What do you know? What are you trying to find? MP.1.1

_____

_____

_____

6. **Make Sense** What hidden question do you need to answer first? Find the answer to the hidden question. MP.1.1, 2.NBT.2.7

7. **Explain** Can the truck travel under the bridge? Show your work. Why does your solution make sense? MP.3.1

Name _____

Follow the Path

Color a path from **Start** to **Finish**. Follow the sums and differences that are even numbers. You can only move up, down, right, or left.

TOPIC 11 | **Fluency Practice Activity**

I can ...
add and subtract within 20.

MAFS.2.OA.2.2

Start								
6 + 6	10 + 8	16 − 8	9 − 0	14 − 4	6 − 2	10 + 10	8 − 3	2 + 7
5 + 4	9 − 4	11 − 9	10 + 5	13 − 5	2 − 1	7 + 9	10 − 9	10 + 9
15 − 8	3 + 10	5 + 1	9 + 8	6 + 8	12 − 5	7 + 7	16 − 9	13 − 8
12 − 9	14 − 7	14 − 6	16 − 7	9 + 9	5 + 6	8 − 6	2 + 5	4 + 7
8 + 9	9 + 6	7 + 5	12 − 8	1 + 7	18 − 9	6 − 0	17 − 9	15 − 7

Finish

Vocabulary Review

Word List
- difference
- hundreds
- mental math
- open number line
- partial differences
- regroup

Understand Vocabulary

Draw a line from each term to its example.

1. hundreds

2. open number line

3. regroup

1 ten = 10 ones

8̲23

4. This open number line is incomplete.
   It needs to show counting back to find
   538 − 115. Write in the missing numbers
   and labels.

Use Vocabulary in Writing

5. Find 235 − 127. Use
   terms from the Word List
   to explain your work.

_____

_____

_____

_____

_____

Name _____

Set A

You can subtract 10 or 100 mentally.

$249 - 10 = ?$

4 tens minus 1 ten is 3 tens.

$249 - 10 = 239$

$249 - 100 = ?$

2 hundreds minus 1 hundred is 1 hundred.

$249 - 100 = 149$

Subtract using place-value blocks or mental math.

1. $426 - 10 = $ _____

2. $345 - 100 = $ _____

3. $287 - 100 = $ _____

4. $309 - 10 = $ _____

5. $800 - 10 = $ _____

6. $140 - 100 = $ _____

Set B

Find $213 - 108$.

One Way
Start at 108 on an open number line. Add up to 213.

Another Way
Count back from 213 on an open number line.

+100   +5
108   208 213

−5 −3   −100
105 110 113   213

So, $213 - 108 = $ __105__.

Use the open number line to subtract.

7. $449 - 217 = $ _____

⟵⟶

8. $903 - 678 = $ _____

⟵⟶

You can draw place-value blocks to show subtraction. Find 327 − 219.

327 − 219 = __108__

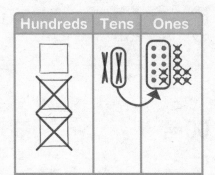

Hundreds	Tens	Ones

Draw blocks to find the partial differences. Record the partial differences to find the difference.

9. 653 − 427 = _____

Hundreds	Tens	Ones

Set D

Thinking Habits

Persevere

What do I know?

What do I need to find?

How can I check that my solution makes sense?

Solve the problem.
Ask yourself questions to help.

10. Marni has 354 pennies. First, she gives 149 pennies to her sister. Then, she gets 210 more pennies from her mother. How many pennies does Marni have now?

Name _____

1. Which equals 100 less than 763?
   Choose all that apply.

   ☐ 663

   ☐ 600 + 60 + 3

   ☐ 863

   ☐ 800 + 60 + 3

   ☐ 600 + 100 + 60

2. The open number line below
   shows subtraction.

   Complete the equation. Write the
   numbers being subtracted and the
   difference.

   _____ − _____ = _____

3. Nico collected 235 coins. Amber
   collected 120 fewer coins than Nico.
   How many coins did they collect in all?

   Ⓐ 350

   Ⓑ 115

   Ⓒ 500

   Ⓓ 550

4. There are 537 boys and 438 girls at the
   concert. How many more boys than girls
   are at the concert?

   Ⓐ 89

   Ⓑ 99

   Ⓒ 101

   Ⓓ 109

5. Show how to add up on an open number line to find $740 - 490$. Then write the difference below.

⟷

$740 - 490 = $ _____

6. Look at your work in Item 5. Explain how you used the number line to find the difference.

_____

_____

_____

_____

_____

_____

_____

7. Use place value and partial differences to find $374 - 157$. Show your work.

$374 - 157 = $ _____

8. Draw place-value blocks to find the difference of $643 - 418$.

Hundreds	Tens	Ones

$643 - 418 = $ _____

Name _____

Bead It!

The chart shows the number of beads sold at Betty's craft store for 4 weeks.

Number of Beads Sold	
Week 1	400
Week 2	536
Week 3	675
Week 4	289

1. How many more beads did Betty sell in Week 2 than in Week 1? Write the missing numbers in the equation. Then use any strategy to solve. 🐊 2.NBT.2.7, MP.4.1

_____ – _____ = _____

_____ more beads

2. 458 glass beads were sold in Week 3. The other beads sold in Week 3 were plastic. How many plastic beads were sold in Week 3? 🐊 2.NBT.2.7, 2.NBT.2.9, MP.3.1, MP.4.1, MP.5.1

Use the open number line to solve.

⟵──────────────────────⟶

_____ – _____ = _____

Explain how you solved the problem. Tell how you know your answer is correct.

[ ]

3. Dex buys 243 beads at Betty's store. He uses 118 of them to make a bracelet. How many beads does Dex have left?

Solve the problem. Show your work. Explain which strategy you used.

 2.NBT.2.7, 2.NBT.2.9, MP.3.1, MP.4.1

_____ – _____ = _____

_____ beads

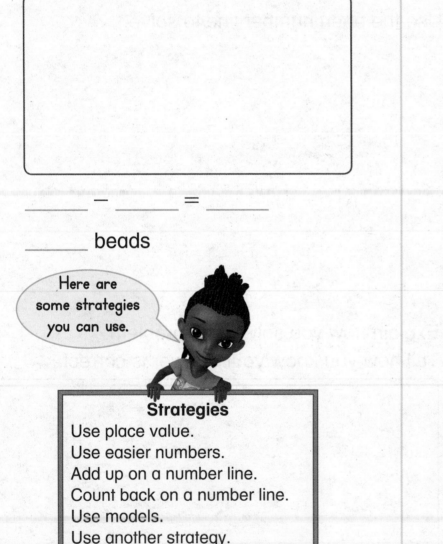

Here are some strategies you can use.

Strategies
Use place value.
Use easier numbers.
Add up on a number line.
Count back on a number line.
Use models.
Use another strategy.

4. Ginny buys 958 beads. 245 beads are blue. 309 beads are orange. 153 beads are white. The rest are red. How many red beads does Ginny buy? 2.NBT.2.7, 2.NBT.2.9, MP.1.1, MP.2.1, MP.3.1

Part A
What is the hidden question in the problem?

_____

_____

Part B
Solve the problem. Show your work. Explain which strategy you used.

_____ red beads

© Pearson Education, Inc. 2

Measuring Length

Essential Question: What are ways to measure length?

Digital Resources

Interactive Student Edition · Activity · Visual Learning · Video · Practice

Assessment · Games · Tools · Glossary

MAFS.2.MD.1.1, 2.MD.1.2, 2.MD.1.3, 2.MD.1.4, 2.MD.2.5

MAFS.K12.MP.1.1, MP.2.1, MP.3.1, MP.4.1, MP.5.1, MP.6.1, MP.7.1, MP.8.1

Look how tall sunflowers grow!

Sunlight and water help plants grow.

Wow! Let's do this project and learn more.

enVision STEM Project: Growing and Measuring

Find Out Grow bean plants. Give them numbers. Put some in sunlight. Put some in a dark place. Water some of the plants. Do not water some of the plants. See how the plants in each group grow.

Journal: Make a Book Show what you learn in a book. In your book, also:

• Tell if plants need sunlight and water to grow.

• Find plants to measure. Draw pictures of the plants. Tell how tall each plant is.

Name _____

Review What You Know

A-Z Vocabulary

1. Draw a line under the bat to show its **length**.

2. School is getting out. Circle **a.m.** or **p.m.**

a.m.

p.m.

3. Draw clock hands to show **quarter past** 10.

Estimating and Measuring Length

4. Use snap cubes.

Estimate the length.

about _____ cubes

Measure the length.

about _____ cubes

5. Use snap cubes.

Estimate the length.

about _____ cubes

Measure the length.

about _____ cubes

Skip Counting

6. Write the missing numbers.

5, 10, _____, 20, _____

210, 220, _____, 240

400, _____, 600, 700

Look for a pattern.

Name _____

PROJECT 12A

How are measurements used to design clothing?

Project: Measure Feet and Create Sock Designs

PROJECT 12B

What units should you use to measure longer distances?

Project: Compare the Measurements of Sports Fields

PROJECT 12C

What can help you remember different measurement facts?

Project: Create a Booklet of Measurement Rhymes

PROJECT 12D

How long or how tall are some animals and insects?

Project: Make a Poster of Snake Lengths

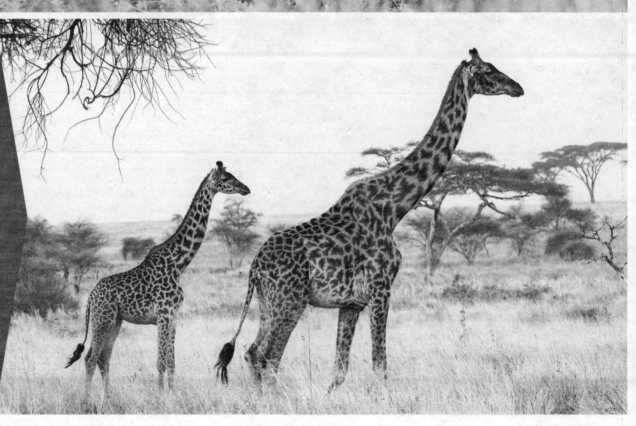

© Pearson Education, Inc. 2

Name _____

Solve & Share

Your thumb is about 1 inch long. Use your thumb to find three objects that are each about 1 inch long. Draw the objects.

From your elbow to your fingers is about 1 foot long. Use this part of your arm to find three objects that are each about 1 foot long. Draw the objects.

I can …
estimate the length of an object by relating the length of the object to a measurement I know.

MAFS.2.MD.1.3 Estimate lengths using units of inches, feet, yards, centimeters, and meters.
MAFS.K12.MP.2.1, MP.6.1

about 1 inch	about 1 foot

You can use the length of objects you know to **estimate** the length of other objects.

Some small paper clips are 1 inch (1 in.) long.

Use a small paper clip to estimate how long the eraser is.

The eraser is about 2 paper clips long. So, it is about 2 inches long.

You can estimate with objects that are about 1 foot (ft) and 1 yard (yd) in length, too.

1 yd

1 ft

Convince Me! Is your height closer to 4 feet or 4 yards? How do you know?

☆**Guided Practice**☆ Write the name and length of an object whose length you know. Then use that object to help you estimate the length of the object shown.

Object	Object Whose Length I Know	Estimate
1. ⟷ (pencil)	My paper clip is _1 inch_ long.	My pencil is about _____ long.
2. (desk)	My _book_ is _____ long.	My desk is about _____ long.

© Pearson Education, Inc. 2

Independent Practice

Write the name and length of an object whose length you know. Then use that object to help you estimate the length of the object shown.

Object	Object Whose Length I Know	Estimate
3.	My _____ is _____ long.	My hand is about _____ long.
4.	My _____ is _____ long.	My chair is about _____ high.

5. **Higher Order Thinking** Would you estimate the distance from your classroom to the principal's office in inches, feet, or yards? How many units? Explain.

_____

_____

_____

_____

A giant step is about a yard.

6. **Ⓐ-z Vocabulary** Complete each sentence using one of the words below.

exact   estimated   inch   yard

An _____ measurement is a good guess.

The height of a kitchen window is about 1 _____.

A small paper clip is about 1 _____ long.

7. **Reasoning** Joy and Kyle estimate the height of their classroom. Joy estimates the height to be 10 feet. Kyle estimates the height to be 10 yards. Who has the better estimate? Explain.

_____

_____

_____

_____

8. **Higher Order Thinking** A city wants to build a bridge over a river. Should they plan out an exact length of the bridge, or is an estimated length good enough? Explain.

_____

_____

_____

_____

9. **🐦 Assessment Practice** Draw a line from each estimate to a matching object. 🐦 2.MD.1.3

| About 1 inch | About 1 foot | About 1 yard |

© Pearson Education, Inc. 2

Name _____

Solve & Share

The orange square is 1 inch long. How can you use 1 inch squares to find the length of the line in inches? Measure the line and explain.

I can ...

estimate measures and use a ruler to measure length and height to the nearest inch.

MAFS.2.MD.1.1 Measure the length of an object to the nearest inch, foot, centimeter, or meter by selecting and using appropriate tools such as rulers, yardsticks, meter sticks, and measuring tapes. **Also 2.MD.1.3** **MAFS.K12.MP.1.1, MP.3.1, MP.5.1**

1 inch

The line is about _____ inches long.

You can measure the length and **height** of an object in inches (in.).

Start measuring from the 0 mark on the ruler.

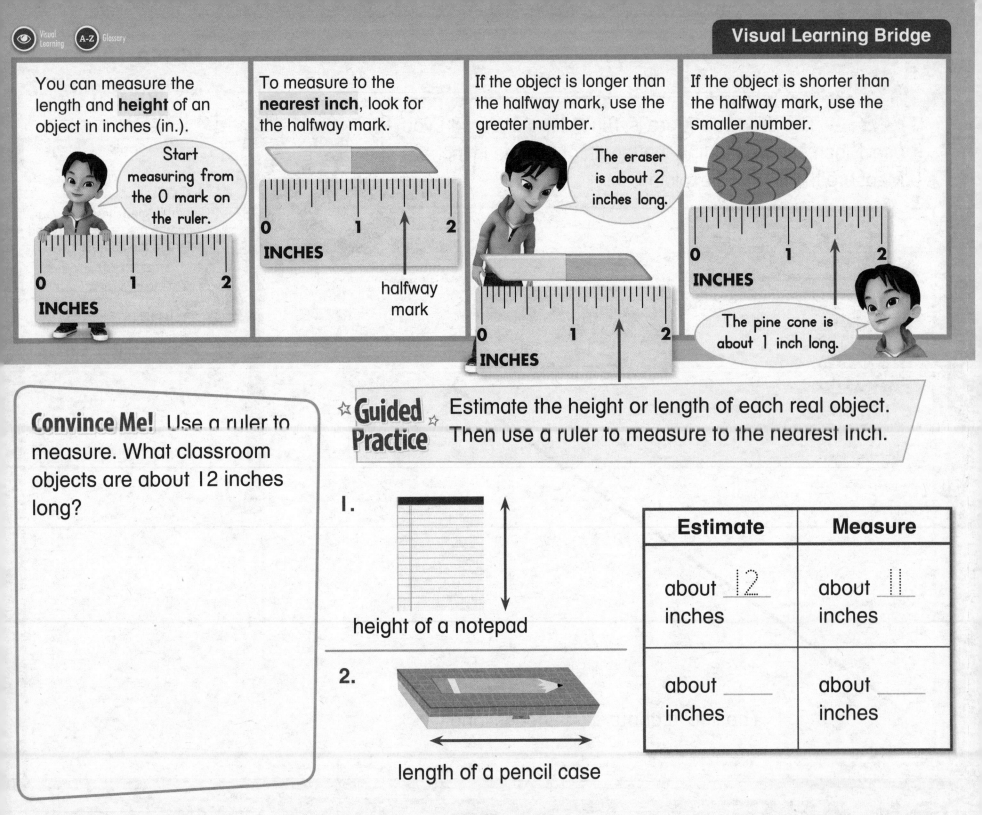

To measure to the **nearest inch**, look for the halfway mark.

halfway mark

If the object is longer than the halfway mark, use the greater number.

The eraser is about 2 inches long.

If the object is shorter than the halfway mark, use the smaller number.

The pine cone is about 1 inch long.

Convince Me! Use a ruler to measure. What classroom objects are about 12 inches long?

☆ **Guided Practice** ☆ Estimate the height or length of each real object. Then use a ruler to measure to the nearest inch.

1.

height of a notepad

2.

length of a pencil case

	Estimate	Measure
1.	about _12_ inches	about _11_ inches
2.	about ____ inches	about ____ inches

© Pearson Education, Inc. 2

Name _____

Independent Practice

Estimate the height or length of each real object. Then use a ruler to measure. Compare your estimate and measurement.

3.

width of a book bag

Estimate	Measure
about ____ inches	about ____ inches
about ____ inches	about ____ inches

4.

length of a paintbrush

5.

height of a cup

Estimate	Measure
about ____ inches	about ____ inches
about ____ inches	about ____ inches

6.

length of a crayon box

Higher Order Thinking Think about how to use a ruler to solve each problem.

7. Jason measures an object. The object is just shorter than the halfway mark between 8 and 9 on his inch ruler. How long is the object?

about ____ inches

8. Gina measures an object. The object is just longer than the halfway mark between 9 and 10 on her inch ruler. How long is the object?

about ____ inches

Topic 12 | Lesson 2

9. **Explain** Pam says that each cherry is about 1 inch wide. Is she correct? Explain.

_____

_____

_____

10. **Vocabulary** Find an object in the classroom that measures about 6 inches. Write a sentence to describe the object. Use these words.

estimate   inches

_____

_____

_____

_____

11. **Higher Order Thinking** Explain how to use an inch ruler to measure the length of an object.

_____

_____

_____

_____

12. **Assessment Practice** Use a ruler. About how many inches long are the two stamps together? 2.MD.1.1

Ⓐ 4 inches   Ⓒ 2 inches

Ⓑ 3 inches   Ⓓ 1 inch

© Pearson Education, Inc. 2
Topic 12 | Lesson 2

Name _____

Solve & Share

Which objects in the classroom are about 1 inch, about 1 foot, and about 1 yard long? Show these objects below.

Activity

I can ...
estimate measures and use tools to measure the length and height of objects to the nearest inch, foot, and yard.

MAFS.2.MD.1.1 Measure the length of an object to the nearest inch, foot, centimeter, or meter by selecting and using appropriate tools such as rulers, yardsticks, meter sticks, and measuring tapes. **Also 2.MD.1.3 MAFS.K12.MP.2.1, MP.5.1, MP.8.1**

about 1 inch

about 1 foot

about 1 yard

You can use a ruler to measure length.

INCHES

The paper clip is about 1 inch (in.).

The book is about 1 foot (ft). 1 foot is 12 inches long.

You can use a yardstick to measure length, too!

The bat is about 1 yard (yd).

A yardstick is 3 feet or 36 inches long.

You can use a measuring tape to measure inches, feet, or yards.

Convince Me! Would you measure the length of a school building in inches or yards? Why?

☆ **Guided Practice** ☆ Match each object with a reasonable estimate of its length.

1.

about 1 yard

Be ready to tell which tool you would use to measure each object.

2.

about 1 inch

3.

about 1 foot

518 five hundred eighteen

Name _____

Independent Practice

Estimate the length of each real object. Choose a ruler, yardstick, or measuring tape to measure. Write the tool you used.

	Estimate	Measure	Tool
4.	about ____ inches	about ____ inches	_____
5.	about ____ feet	about ____ feet	_____
6.	about ____ yards	about ____ yards	_____

7. **Higher Order Thinking** Explain how you could use a foot ruler to measure the length of a room in feet.

_____

_____

_____

8. **Generalize** Circle the real object that is about 4 feet in length.

9. **Number Sense** Explain how to use a yardstick to measure the length of an object. Estimate the length of your classroom in yards. Then measure.

_____

_____

_____

_____

10. **Higher Order Thinking** Find an object in the classroom that you estimate measures about 2 feet. Draw the object.

What tool would you use to measure it? Explain why you chose the tool you did.

_____

11. **Assessment Practice** Jon sets two of the same real objects next to each other. Together, they have a length of about 4 feet. Which is the object Jon uses? 2.MD.1.3

Ⓐ MATH

Ⓒ

Ⓑ

Ⓓ

Name _____

Solve & Share

Choose an object. Measure your object in feet. Then measure it in inches.

Do you need more units of feet or inches to measure your object? Why?

I can ...
estimate and measure the length and height of objects in inches, feet, and yards.

MAFS.2.MD.1.2 Describe the inverse relationship between the size of a unit and number of units needed to measure a given object. . . . Also 2.MD.1.1
MAFS.K12.MP.3.1, MP.5.1, MP.6.1

about _____ feet long

about _____ inches long

_____

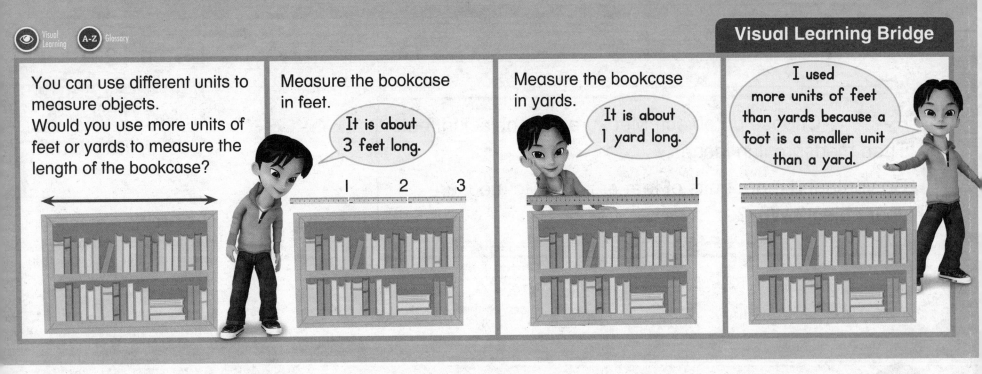

You can use different units to measure objects.
Would you use more units of feet or yards to measure the length of the bookcase?

Measure the bookcase in feet.

It is about 3 feet long.

Measure the bookcase in yards.

It is about 1 yard long.

I used more units of feet than yards because a foot is a smaller unit than a yard.

Convince Me! Juan measures the height of a wall in his room. He lines the wall with one-foot rulers. He could find this height with yardsticks. Would Juan need more rulers or yardsticks? Explain.

☆ **Guided Practice** ☆ Measure each real object using different units. Circle the unit you use *more* of to measure each object.

1. about _____ feet   about _____ yards

I use more units of:

feet   yards

2. about _____ inches   about _____ feet

I use more units of:

inches   feet

Topic 12 | Lesson 4

Name _____

Independent Practice

Measure each real object using different units.
Circle the unit you use *fewer* of to measure each object.

3.

A Bear's Life

about _____ inches   about _____ feet

I use fewer units of:

inches   feet

5.

about _____ feet

about _____ yards

I use fewer units of:

feet   yards

4.

about _____ feet   about _____ yards

I use fewer units of:

feet   yards

Number Sense Circle the best estimate for the length of each object.

6. About how long is a key?

2 inches   2 feet   2 yards

Which tool would you use to measure the length of a key?

_____

7. About how long is a suitcase?

2 inches   2 feet   2 yards

Which tool would you use to measure the length of a suitcase?

_____

Problem Solving ★ Solve each problem.

8. **Use Tools** Measure the length of an object in your classroom using two different units.

Object: _____

about _____ about _____

Which unit did you use more of? _____

Circle which tool you used.

ruler   yardstick   measuring tape

9. **Higher Order Thinking** Andrew wants to measure the length of a football field. Should he use feet or yards to measure it? Which tool should he use? Explain.

_____

_____

_____

_____

_____

10. 🐊 **Assessment Practice** Which unit would you need the fewest of to measure the length of the table? 🐊 2.MD.1.2

Ⓐ inches   Ⓒ yards

Ⓑ feet   Ⓓ all the same

11. 🐊 **Assessment Practice** Which is the best estimate for the length of a vegetable garden? 🐊 2.MD.1.2

Ⓐ about 5 inches   Ⓒ about 5 yards

Ⓑ about 1 foot   Ⓓ about 20 inches

                   Topic 12 | Lesson 4

Name _____

Solve & Share

The green cube is 1 centimeter long. How can you use 1 centimeter cubes to find the length of the line in centimeters? Measure the line and explain.

I can ...
estimate measures and use a ruler to measure length and height to the nearest centimeter.

MAFS.2.MD.1.1 Measure the length of an object to the nearest inch, foot, centimeter, or meter by selecting and using appropriate tools such as rulers, yardsticks, meter sticks, and measuring tapes. Also 2.MD.1.3 MAFS.K12.MP.3.1, MP.6.1, MP.7.1

1 cm

The line is about _____ centimeters long.

I **centimeter (cm)** is smaller than 1 inch.

INCHES
CENTIMETERS

I cm

Start measuring from the 0 mark. To measure to the **nearest centimeter**, look for the halfway mark. If the object is longer than the halfway mark, use the greater number.

The cube is about 2 centimeters long.

CENTIMETERS

halfway mark

If the object is shorter than the halfway mark, use the smaller number.

CENTIMETERS

This paper clip is about 3 centimeters long.

Convince Me! Explain how you know the length of the paper clip above is about 3 centimeters long.

☆ **Guided Practice** ☆ Estimate the height or length of each real object. Use a ruler to measure to the nearest centimeter.

1.

length of a stapler

2.

height of a book

Estimate	Measure
about 15 centimeters	about 18 centimeters
about ___ centimeters	about ___ centimeters

© Pearson Education, Inc. 2

Name _____

Independent Practice

Estimate the width, height, or length of each real object.
Then use a ruler to measure. Compare your estimate and measurement.

3.

width of
a shoelace

Estimate	Measure
about _____ centimeters	about _____ centimeters
about _____ centimeters	about _____ centimeters

4.

width of
a chair

5.

length of
a pencil

Estimate	Measure
about _____ centimeters	about _____ centimeters
about _____ centimeters	about _____ centimeters

6.

height of
scissors

Higher Order Thinking Explain whether each estimate is reasonable or not.

7. Josh estimated that the length of his reading book is about 6 centimeters.

_____

_____

8. Shae estimated that the height of her desk is about 10 centimeters.

_____

_____

9. (A-Z) **Vocabulary** Find an object that is about 10 centimeters long.
Write a sentence to describe your object using these words.

centimeters   **estimate**

_____

_____

_____

10. **Look for Patterns** Nick wants to put another pen end to end with this one. About how long would the two pens be together?

about _____ centimeters

11. **Higher Order Thinking** Paul says that a toothbrush is about 19 centimeters long. Sarah says it is about 50 centimeters long. Who is correct? Explain.

_____

_____

_____

12. 🏴 **Assessment Practice** Mary measures the length of her eraser to the nearest centimeter. What is the length of her eraser to the nearest centimeter? (📷) 2.MD.1.1

_____ centimeters

Name _____

Solve & Share

Which objects in the classroom are about 3 centimeters long?
Which objects are about 1 meter long?
Show these objects below.

I can ...
estimate measures and use a ruler, a meter stick, or a tape measure to measure length and height to the nearest centimeter or meter.

MAFS.2.MD.1.1 Measure the length of an object to the nearest inch, foot, centimeter, or meter by selecting and using appropriate tools such as rulers, yardsticks, meter sticks, and measuring tapes. Also 2.MD.1.3 MAFS.K12.MP.3.1, MP.5.1, MP.6.1

about 3 centimeters

about 1 meter

You can use a ruler or a meter stick to measure length.

1 meter is 100 centimeters long!

meter stick

ruler

The button is about 1 centimeter (cm) long.

CENTIMETERS
0 1 2 3 4 5

This table is about 1 meter (m) wide.

1 m

You can also use a measuring tape to measure centimeters and meters.

Convince Me! Would you measure the length of a house in centimeters or meters? Why?

☆ **Guided Practice** ☆ Match each object with a reasonable estimate of its length.

1. ↔ 	about 1 cm

2. 🚚 	about 10 cm

3. 🪑 	about 1 m

4. 🖍️ 	about 10 m

Think about which tool you would use to measure each object.

© Pearson Education, Inc. 2

Name _____

Independent Practice

Estimate the length or height of each real object shown. Then choose a tool and measure. Compare your estimate and measurement.

	Estimate	Measure	Tool
5.	about _____ cm	about _____ cm	_____
6.	about _____ m	about _____ m	_____
7.	about _____ cm	about _____ cm	_____
8.	about _____ m	about _____ m	_____

9. Tom uses a meter stick to measure the length of a fence. He places the meter stick 5 times on the fence to measure from one end to the other end. How long is the fence?

_____ meters

10. **Higher Order Thinking** Debbie says that her doll is about 30 meters long. Do you think this is a good estimate? Why or why not?

_____

_____

11. Be Precise Choose an object to measure. Use metric units. Estimate first and then measure.
Draw the object and write your estimate and measurement. Was your estimate reasonable?

Remember to include the units.

12. Circle the real object that would be about 2 meters long.

13. Higher Order Thinking Each side of a place-value cube is 1 centimeter long. Use a place-value cube to draw a 5-centimeter ruler.

14. 🌀 **Assessment Practice** Choose an appropriate tool. Measure each line. Which lines are at least 6 centimeters long? Choose all that apply. 🌀 2.MD.1.1

Solve & Share

Measure this pencil in inches. Then measure it again in centimeters. Which measurement has more units?

Lesson 12-7
Measure Length Using Different Metric Units

I can ...
measure the length and height of objects using different metric units.

MAFS.2.MD.1.2 Describe the inverse relationship between the size of a unit and number of units needed to measure a given object. . . . Also 2.MD.1.1
MAFS.K12.MP.2.1, MP.3.1, MP.6.1

about _____ inches   about _____ centimeters

Which has more units? _____

You can use different units to measure the lengths of objects. Would you use more units of centimeters or meters to measure the desk?

Measure the length using centimeters.

It is about 91 centimeters long!

Measure the length using meters.

It is about 1 meter long!

I used more units of centimeters than meters because a centimeter is a much smaller unit than a meter.

Convince Me! Tina measures the length of a room with centimeter rulers. She could find this length with meter sticks. Would Tina need fewer rulers or meter sticks? Explain.

Guided Practice Measure each real object using different units. Circle the unit you use *more* of to measure each object.

1.
   about _____ centimeters

   about _____ meters

   I use more units of: centimeters   meters

2.
   about _____ centimeters

   about _____ meters

   I use more units of: centimeters   meters

© Pearson Education, Inc. 2

Topic 12 | Lesson 7

Independent Practice Measure each real object using different units.
Circle the unit you use *fewer* of to measure each object.

3.

about _____ meters   about _____ centimeters

I use fewer units of: centimeters   meters

4.

about _____ meters   about _____ centimeters

I use fewer units of: centimeters   meters

5. **Higher Order Thinking** Jay measured the height of his bedroom in both centimeters and meters. Did he use fewer units of centimeters or meters? Explain.

_____

_____

_____

_____

6. Explain If you had to measure the length of the hallway outside of your classroom, would you use centimeters or meters? Explain.

_____

_____

_____

7. Higher Order Thinking A meter stick is about 39 inches long. Is a meter longer or shorter than a yard? Explain.

_____

_____

_____

_____

8. 🔊 **Assessment Practice** Estimate the length of a baseball bat in centimeters and meters. 🔊 2.MD.1.2

_____ centimeters

_____ meters

Which number must be greater? Explain.

_____

_____

_____

_____

9. 🔊 **Assessment Practice** Tina measures the length of a jump rope using different units. How will her measurements compare? 🔊 2.MD.1.2

Choose Yes or No.

More units of meters than centimeters ◯ Yes ◯ No

More units of inches than feet ◯ Yes ◯ No

More units of yards than feet ◯ Yes ◯ No

Name _____

Solve & Share

Circle two paths. Estimate which one is longer. How can you check if your estimate is correct?

I can ...
tell how much longer one object is than another.

MAFS.2.MD.1.4 Measure to determine how much longer one object is than another, expressing the length difference in terms of a standard length unit. Also 2.MD.2.5 MAFS.K12.MP.2.1, MP.3.1, MP.4.1

Estimate: The _____ path is longer.

Measure: The _____ path is longer.

Which path is longer? How much longer?

Think about both parts of the path when you estimate and measure.

Estimate: _5_ cm

Estimate: _6_ cm

One part of the blue path is about 2 cm. The other part is about 2 cm. Add to find the length.

$2 + 2 = 4$
The blue path is about 4 cm long.

CENTIMETERS
0 1 2 3 4

One part of the red path is about 1 cm. The other part is about 4 cm. Add to find the length.

$1 + 4 = 5$
The red path is about 5 cm long.

CENTIMETERS

Subtract to compare lengths.
$5 - 4 = 1$

The red path is about 1 cm longer than the blue path.

Convince Me! How can you find the length of a path that is not straight?

☆ **Guided Practice** ☆   Estimate the length of each path. Then use a centimeter ruler to measure each path.

1.   Path A

Estimate: about _9_ cm

Measure: about _10_ cm

2.   Path B

Estimate: about ____ cm

Measure: about ____ cm

3. Which path is longer?

_____

4. How much longer?

about ____ cm longer

© Pearson Education, Inc. 2

Name _____

Independent Practice

Estimate the length of each path. Then use a centimeter ruler to measure each path. Compare your estimate and measurement.

5.

Path C

Estimate: about _____ centimeters

Measure: about _____ centimeters

6.

Path D

Estimate: about _____ centimeters

Measure: about _____ centimeters

7. Which path is longer?

_____

8. How much longer?

about _____ centimeters longer

Higher Order Thinking Think about the length of each object. Circle the best estimate of its length.

9. a key

about 1 cm   about 6 cm   about 20 cm

Think about objects that are about 1 cm long to help.

10. a pen

about 2 cm   about 4 cm   about 15 cm

Use your estimates to complete:

A pen is about _____ cm

_____ than a key.

11. Explain A path has two parts. The total length of the path is 12 cm. If one part is 8 cm, how long is the other part? Explain.

_____ centimeters

12. Higher Order Thinking Draw a path with two parts. Measure the length to the nearest centimeter. Write an equation to show the length of your path.

13. Higher Order Thinking Beth drew a picture of a bike path. Use tools. Measure the length of the path below. Write the total length.

Beth's Path

about _____ centimeters

14. 🔄 **Assessment Practice** Measure each path in centimeters.

Path A

Path B

How much longer is Path A than Path B? Show your work. 🔄 2.MD.1.4

_____

_____

_____

© Pearson Education, Inc. 2

Name _____

Solve & Share

Zeke measures the snake and says it is about 4 inches long. Jay says it is about 5 inches long.

Who measures the snake more precisely? Measure and explain.

I can ...
choose tools, units, and methods that help me be precise when I measure.

MAFS.K12.MP.6.1 Attend to precision. **Also** MP.1.1, MP.3.1, MP.5.1
MAFS.2.MD.1.1 Measure the length of an object to the nearest inch, foot, centimeter, or meter by selecting and using appropriate tools such as rulers, yardsticks, meter sticks, and measuring tapes. Also 2.MD.1.3, 2.MD.1.4

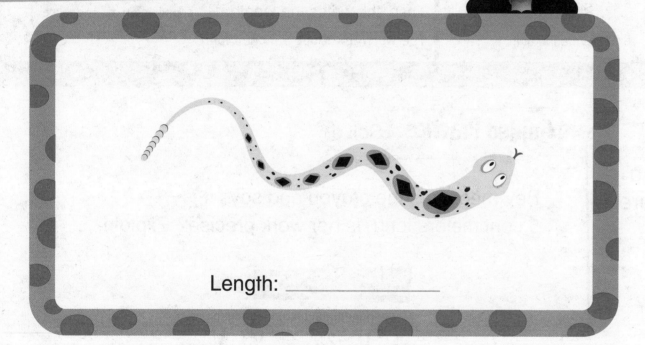

Length: _____

Thinking Habits
Which unit of measure will I use?

Is my work precise?

_____
_____
_____

Anna uses a string to help measure the worm.

Is her work precise? Why or why not?

What can I do to measure precisely?

I can choose units and tools that will help me measure precisely.

Measure Precisely
Estimate first.
Choose a tool.
Start at 0.
Measure twice.
Write the unit.

Anna lines up the string along a ruler to measure the length.

0   1   2   3
INCHES

Then Anna measures the worm again to check her work. Then she writes the length.

The worm is about 3 inches long.

Anna uses precision to measure and write the units.

Convince Me! How does using a string help Anna use precision to measure the worm?

⭐ **Guided Practice**   Solve.

1. Bev measures the crayon and says it is 5 centimeters long. Is her work precise? Explain.

0   1   2   3   4   5
CENTIMETERS

Name _____

Independent Practice ☆ Solve each problem.

2. Steve uses centimeter cubes. He says the pencil is 9 centimeters long. Is his work precise? Explain.

_____

_____

3. Use a centimeter ruler to measure the pencil yourself. How long is the pencil? Explain what you did to make sure your work is precise.

_____

_____

_____

4. Find the difference in the lengths of the paths in inches. Is your answer precise? Explain.

_____

_____

_____

Problem Solving

Shoestring

Katie lost a shoestring.
The shoestring has the same length as the
shoestring at the right.
What is the length of the shoestring Katie lost?

5. **Make Sense** Estimate the length of the
shoestring in the picture. Explain how your
estimate helps you measure. 2.MD.1.3, MP.1.1

_____

_____

_____

6. **Use Tools** What tools can you use
to measure the shoestring? Explain. MP.5.1

_____

_____

_____

_____

7. **Be Precise** Measure the shoestring.
Tell why your work is precise. 2.MD.1.1, MP.6.1

_____

_____

© Pearson Education, Inc. 2

Find a Match

Find a partner. Point to a clue. Read the clue.

Look below the clues to find a match. Write the clue letter in the box next to the match.

Find a match for every clue.

I can ...
add and subtract within 100.

MAFS.2.NBT.2.5

Clues

A The sum is between 47 and 53.

B The difference equals 56 − 20.

C The sum equals 100.

D The difference equals 79 − 27.

E The difference is between 25 and 35.

F The sum equals 41 + 56.

G The difference is less than 20.

H The sum equals 26 + 19.

☐ 81 − 29	☐ 60 − 24	☐ 34 + 11	☐ 23 + 27
☐ 63 − 34	☐ 32 + 65	☐ 56 + 44	☐ 47 − 31

Understand Vocabulary

1. Circle the unit that has the *greatest* length.

foot   meter   inch

2. Circle the unit that has the *shortest* length.

yard   inch   centimeter

3. Cross out the unit you would **NOT** use to measure the length of a book.

inch   centimeter   yard

4. Cross out the unit you would **NOT** use to measure the height of a house.

inch   foot   meter

Word List

- centimeter (cm)
- estimate
- foot (ft)
- height
- inch (in.)
- length
- meter (m)
- nearest centimeter
- nearest inch
- yard (yd)

A-Z Glossary

Estimate the length of each item.

5. pencil

6. paper clip

7. school desk

Use Vocabulary in Writing

8. Use words to tell how to find the height of a table. Use terms from the Word List.

Name _____

Set A _____

There are 12 inches in 1 foot.
There are 3 feet in 1 yard.
You can use lengths of objects you know to estimate lengths of other objects.

about 1 inch

about 1 foot

about 1 yard

Estimate the lengths of two classroom objects in feet. Name each object and write your estimate.

1. Object: _____

   about _____ feet

2. Object: _____

   about _____ feet

Set B _____

You can measure the length of an object to the nearest inch.

INCHES

halfway mark

The string is longer than halfway between 1 and 2.
So, use the greater number.
The string is about _2_ inches.

Find objects like the ones shown. Use a ruler to measure their lengths.

3.

   about _____ inches

4.

   about _____ inches

The measure of the height of a window takes *more* units of feet than yards.

about ⌐3 feet

about ⌐1 yard

Measure the real object in inches and feet. Circle the unit you needed *more* of.

5.

about _____ feet

about _____ yards

feet   yards

You can measure the length of an object to the nearest centimeter.

The paper clip is less than halfway between 3 and 4.
So, use the lesser number.
The paper clip is about ⌐3 cm.

Find real objects like the ones shown. Use a ruler to measure their lengths.

6.

about _____ cm

7.

about _____ cm

© Pearson Education, Inc. 2

Name _____

Set E

There are 100 centimeters in 1 meter.

about 1 centimeter

about 1 meter

Circle the picture of the real object that is about each length or height.

8. about 1 centimeter

9. about 1 meter

Set F

The measure of the height of this cart takes *fewer* units of meters than centimeters.

about _93_ centimeters

about _1_ meter

Measure the real object in centimeters and meters. Circle the unit you needed *fewer* of.

10. about _____ centimeters

about _____ meters

centimeters

meters

Which path is longer? How much longer?
Measure each part. Then add the lengths.

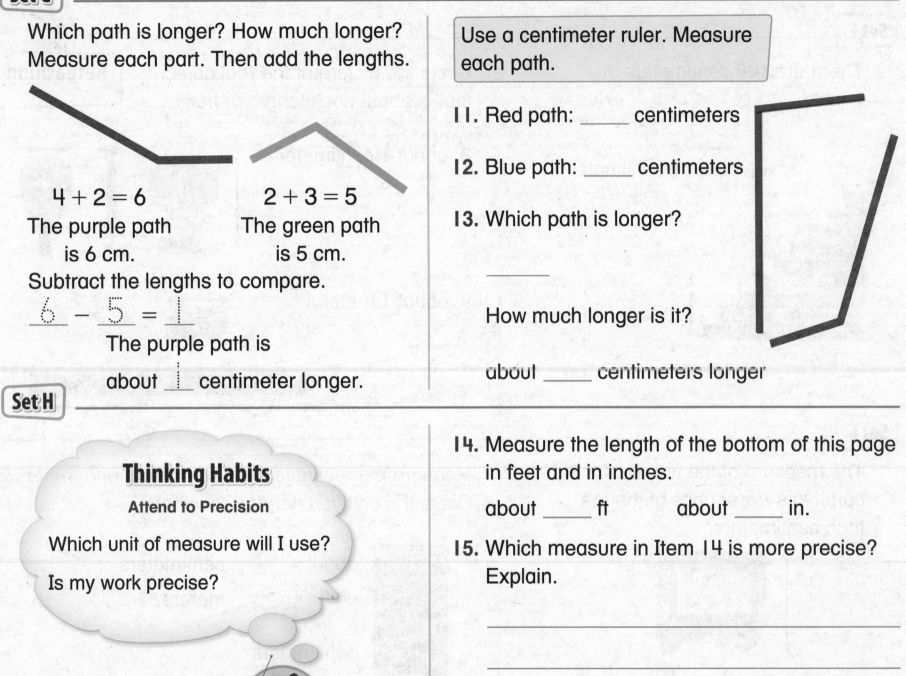

$4 + 2 = 6$

The purple path
is 6 cm.

$2 + 3 = 5$

The green path
is 5 cm.

Subtract the lengths to compare.

$\underline{6} - \underline{5} = \underline{1}$

The purple path is

about $\underline{1}$ centimeter longer.

Use a centimeter ruler. Measure each path.

11. Red path: _____ centimeters

12. Blue path: _____ centimeters

13. Which path is longer?

_____

How much longer is it?

about _____ centimeters longer

Thinking Habits

Attend to Precision

Which unit of measure will I use?

Is my work precise?

14. Measure the length of the bottom of this page in feet and in inches.

about _____ ft   about _____ in.

15. Which measure in Item 14 is more precise? Explain.

_____

_____

_____

© Pearson Education, Inc. 2   **Topic 12** | Reteaching

Name _____

1. Estimate. About how tall is the flower?

Ⓐ about 5 cm

Ⓑ about 10 cm

Ⓒ about 15 cm

Ⓓ about 1 meter

1 cm

2. Draw a line from each estimate to a matching object.

about 1 yard

about 1 foot

about 1 inch

3. Which units would you need the fewest of to measure the height of a fence?

Ⓐ inches

Ⓑ feet

Ⓒ yards

Ⓓ all the same

4. Dan measures the width of a window with a yardstick. He says it measures 3. Is his answer precise? Explain.

_____

_____

_____

5. Use a ruler to measure each line to the nearest centimeter.
Which are about 3 centimeters long? Choose all that apply.

☐ none of them

6. Use a ruler to measure the length of the pencil in inches.
Which is the correct measurement?

Ⓐ 2 inches   Ⓒ 4 inches

Ⓑ 3 inches   Ⓓ 5 inches

7. Circle the unit you need fewer of to measure the length of a kitchen.

centimeters   meters

Circle the unit you need fewer of to measure the length of a table.

feet   yards

8. Use a ruler. Measure each path to the nearest inch.

Which path is longer? _____

How much longer? about _____ longer

Name _____

9. Use a ruler. Measure the length of the
marker to the nearest centimeter.
How long is the marker?

Ⓐ 6 centimeters Ⓒ 12 centimeters

Ⓑ 9 centimeters Ⓓ 15 centimeters

10. A path has two parts.
The total length of the path
is 15 cm.
One part of the path is 9 cm long.
How long is the other part?

Ⓐ 24 cm

Ⓑ 15 cm

Ⓒ 9 cm

Ⓓ 6 cm

11. Use a ruler. Measure each path to the
nearest centimeter.

Path A

Path B

Which path is longer? _____

How much longer?

about _____ longer

12. Measure the gray line with tools you need
to be precise. Choose all the measurements
that are precise.

☐ 4 centimeters

☐ 4 inches

☐ 10

☐ 10 centimeters

☐ 4

13. Juan uses different units to measure a jump rope. Compare the measurements. Choose all that apply.

☐ more inches than feet

☐ fewer centimeters than meters

☐ fewer inches than feet

☐ more yards than feet

☐ more centimeters than meters

☐ fewer yards than feet

14. What is the length of the crayon to the nearest centimeter? What would be the combined length of two crayons?

The crayon is _____ centimeters.

Two crayons would measure _____ centimeters.

15. Kim's softball bat is 1 yard long. She uses 3 bats to measure the length of the classroom whiteboard. About how long is the whiteboard?

3 inches   3 feet   1 yard   3 yards

Ⓐ   Ⓑ   Ⓒ   Ⓓ

16. Kevin measured the length of a car in inches and in feet. Why is the number of feet less than the number of inches?

96 inches or 8 feet

Name _____

Happy Hiking!

The Torres family loves to hike.

They use this map to plan their hiking trip.

START

Tower

Bridge

1. Use a centimeter ruler.
   Find the total length of the triangle
   hiking path shown on the map.

   about _____ centimeters

   Explain how you found the length.

   🌀 2.MD.1.1, 2.MD.2.5, MP.3.1, MP.5.1

   _____

   _____

   _____

2. Debbie Torres uses a backpack
   for hiking.
   She wants to measure its width.
   She wants to be precise. Should she
   use inches, feet, or yards?
   Explain your answer. 🌀 2.MD.1.1, MP.3.1, MP.6.1

Width of a backpack

_____

_____

_____

_____

3. Daniel Torres estimates the height of his water bottle. Is his estimate reasonable? Explain. 🌀 2.MD.1.3, MP.2.1, MP.3.1

about 20 meters

_____

_____

_____

4. Maria Torres says that it would take more units of yards than feet to measure the height of the tower. Do you agree? Circle Yes or No. Explain. 🌀 2.MD.1.2, MP.3.1

Yes   No

_____

_____

_____

5. On the hike, the Torres family sees a caterpillar. Use the picture below to answer the questions. 🌀 2.MD.1.1, 2.MD.1.3, MP.3.1, MP.6.1

Part A

To be precise, which unit would you choose to measure the length of the caterpillar? Explain.

_____

_____

Part B

Estimate and then measure the length of the caterpillar. Then explain how you measured.

> Estimate: _____
>
> Measurement: _____

_____

_____

_____

TOPIC 13 Shapes and Their Attributes

Essential Question: How can shapes be described, compared, and broken into parts?

Digital Resources

Interactive Student Edition · Activity · Visual Learning · Video · Practice

Assessment · Games · Tools · Glossary

Different tools have different shapes!

How does the shape of a tool help it work?

Wow! Let's do this project and learn more.

MAFS.2.OA.2.2, 2.OA.3.4, 2.MD.1.1, 2.MD.1.2, 2.G.1.1, 2.G.1.2, 2.G.1.3
MAFS.K12. MP.1.1, MP.2.1, MP.3.1, MP.4.1, MP.5.1, MP.6.1, MP.7.1, MP.8.1

enVision STEM Project: All About Shape

Find Out Draw pictures of tools used for gardening, cooking, or fixing. Describe the shape of each tool. Tell how the shape of each tool helps it work.

Journal: Make a Book Show your work in a book. In your book, also:

• Choose a tool that you use at school. Tell how the shape of the tool helps it work.

• Draw and describe polygon shapes.

Name _____

(A-Z) Vocabulary

1. Circle the shape that has 6 **sides**.

2. Circle each **plane shape**. Put a box around each **solid figure**.

3. Put a box around the circle that shows **fourths**.

Basic Facts

4. Write each sum.

5	7	10
+8	+7	+10

5. Write each difference.

17	15	12
−9	−6	−8

Math Story

6. Edna has a bookcase with 5 shelves. She places 5 books in a row on each shelf. Write an equation that shows how many books Edna has in all.

_____

_____

© Pearson Education, Inc. 2

Name _____

PROJECT 13A

What shapes can you find in a tile design?

Project: Create a Tile Design

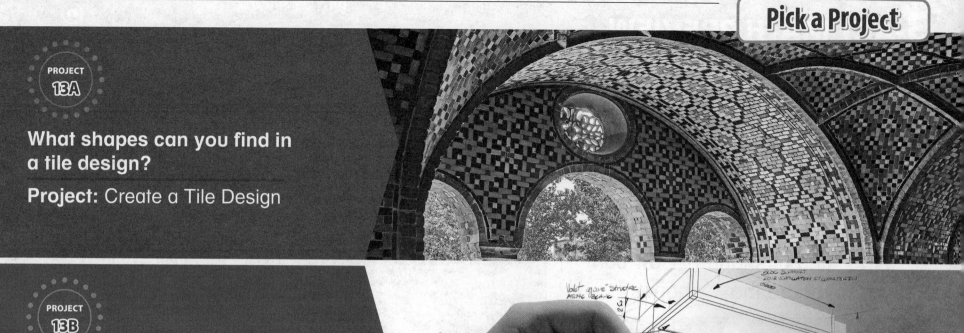

PROJECT 13B

How do architects design a house?

Project: Draw Your Dream Building

PROJECT 13C

What national landmarks are in your state?

Project: Build a Landmark

Math Modeling

Straw Shaped

Video

Before watching the video, think:

What can you build with straws? What kind of shapes? How can you compare those shapes?

MAFS.K12.MP.4.1 Model with mathematics. **Also MP.5.1, MP.7.1**
MAFS.2.MD.1.4 Measure to determine how much longer one object is than another, expressing the length difference in terms of a standard length unit.
Also 2.MD.1.1, 2.MD.2.5, 2.G.1.1

Activity

Solve & Share

Look at the picture.
How many triangles can you find?
Trace each triangle.
Be ready to explain how you know you have found them all.

I can ...
recognize shapes by how they look.

MAFS.2.G.1.1 Recognize and draw shapes having specified attributes, such as a given number of angles or a given number of equal faces. Identify triangles, quadrilaterals, pentagons, hexagons, and cubes. **Also 2.OA.2.2**
MAFS.K12.MP.3.1, MP.4.1, MP.6.1

_____ triangles

Triangles

side

vertex

3 sides, 3 **vertices**

Not Triangles

Quadrilaterals

4 sides, 4 vertices

Not Quadrilaterals

Pentagons

5 sides, 5 vertices

Not Pentagons

Hexagons

6 sides, 6 vertices

Not Hexagons

Convince Me! How do sides and vertices help you name a plane shape?

☆ **Guided Practice** Match each shape to its name.

1.

triangle   quadrilateral   pentagon   hexagon

Tell how many sides and vertices. Name each shape.

2.   _____ sides

                            _____ vertices

Shape: _____

3.   _____ sides

                            _____ vertices

Shape: _____

© Pearson Education, Inc. 2   **Topic 13** | Lesson 1

Name _____

Independent Practice Match each shape to its name.

4.

triangle quadrilateral pentagon hexagon

5.

triangle quadrilateral pentagon hexagon

Draw the shape. Tell how many sides and vertices.

6. Quadrilateral

_____ sides

_____ vertices

7. Hexagon

_____ sides

_____ vertices

8. Triangle

_____ sides

_____ vertices

9. Higher Order Thinking Bianca drew a triangle and a pentagon. How many sides and vertices did she draw in all? Draw the shapes.

_____ sides   _____ vertices

Problem Solving☆ Solve each problem.

10. **Model** Marcos has 4 toothpicks. He places them as shown. What shape can Marcos make if he adds one more toothpick?

_____

11. 🅐🅩 **Vocabulary** Connect all the dots to make two shapes that have **vertices.** Name the shapes that you make.

• • •

• •

• • • •

_____ _____

12. **Higher Order Thinking** Randall said that a square is a quadrilateral. Susan said that a square is a square, so it is not a quadrilateral. Who is correct? Explain.

_____

_____

_____

_____

13. 📝 **Assessment Practice** Which shape is **NOT** a hexagon? 📝 2.G.1.1

Ⓐ

Ⓑ

Ⓒ

Ⓓ

Think: What do I know about hexagons?

© Pearson Education, Inc. 2

Solve & Share

Look at the three plane shapes below. How are they alike? How are they different?

Measure the length of the sides to help describe them. Name each shape.

Activity

Lesson 13-2
Polygons and Angles

I can ...
describe plane shapes by how they look.

MAFS.2.G.1.1 Recognize and draw shapes having specified attributes, such as a given number of angles or a given number of equal faces. Identify triangles, quadrilaterals, pentagons, hexagons, and cubes. **Also 2.MD.1.1**
MAFS.K12.MP.2.1, MP.6.1, MP.7.1

_____   _____   _____

_____

_____

_____

_____

Polygon

A closed plane shape with 3 or more sides is called a polygon.

You know the names of these polygons.

Not Polygons

Polygons are not open shapes. Polygons do not have curved sides.

A circle is not a polygon.

Angle

Polygons have angles. They have the same number of angles as sides and vertices.

A triangle has 3 angles.

Right Angle

A right angle forms a square corner. A square has 4 right angles. The pentagon below has 3 right angles.

Convince Me! How many angles does this shape have? How many right angles? Name the shape.

☆ **Guided Practice** ☆ Write the number of angles and then name the shape.

1.

_____ angles

Shape: _____

2.

_____ angles

Shape: _____

3.

_____ angles

Shape: _____

4.

_____ angles

Shape: _____

Name _____

★ Independent Practice ★ Write the number of angles and then name the shape.

5. 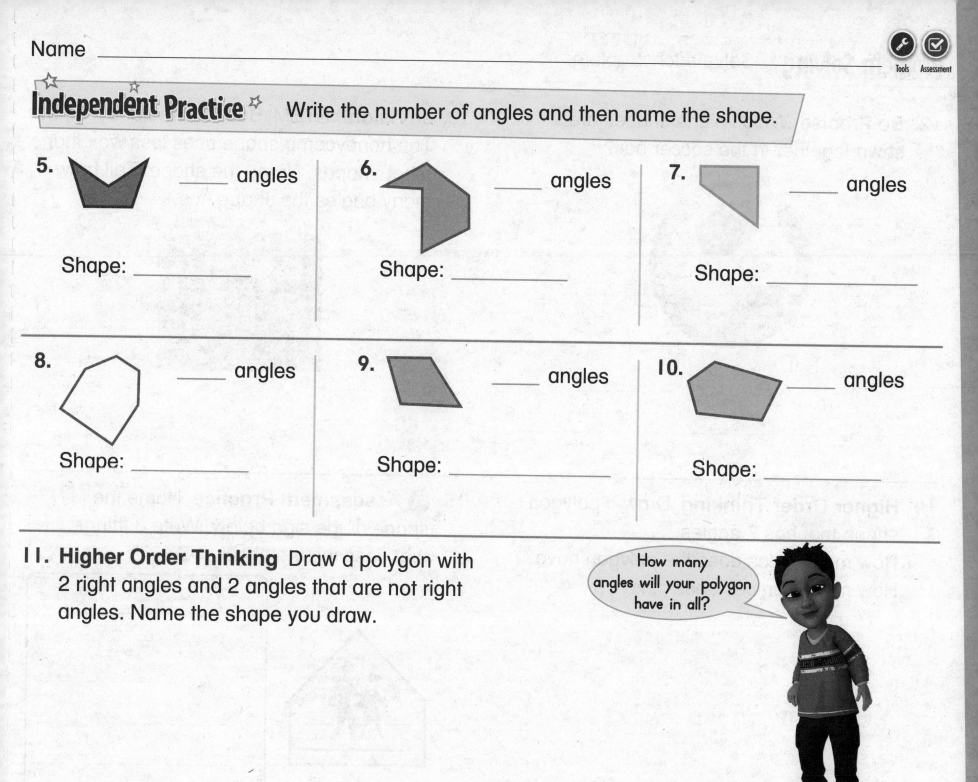 _____ angles

Shape: _____

6. _____ angles

Shape: _____

7. _____ angles

Shape: _____

8. _____ angles

Shape: _____

9. _____ angles

Shape: _____

10. _____ angles

Shape: _____

11. Higher Order Thinking Draw a polygon with 2 right angles and 2 angles that are not right angles. Name the shape you draw.

How many angles will your polygon have in all?

12. Be Precise Which plane shapes are sewn together in the soccer ball?

_____

_____

13. enVision® STEM Bees make honeycomb. The honeycomb shape uses less wax than other shapes. Name the shape. Tell how many angles the shape has.

_____

_____

14. Higher Order Thinking Draw a polygon shape that has 7 angles.
How many sides does the polygon have?
How many vertices does it have?

15. 🏴 **Assessment Practice** Name the shape of the sign below. Write 3 things that describe the shape. 🏴 2.G.1.1

_____

_____

_____

_____

Name _____

Solve & Share

Draw a polygon with 3 sides that are the same length. Then draw a polygon with 3 sides that are different lengths.

Measure the lengths of the sides you drew.
Tell 4 ways the shapes are alike.

I can ...
draw polygon shapes.

MAFS.2.G.1.1 Recognize and draw shapes having specified attributes, such as a given number of angles or a given number of equal faces. Identify triangles, quadrilaterals, pentagons, hexagons, and cubes. Also 2.MD.1.1
MAFS.K12.MP.1.1, MP.6.1, MP.7.1

Sides: Same Length

Sides: Different Lengths

_____

_____

_____

Draw a polygon with 5 vertices.

My polygon will have 5 vertices. That means it will have 5 sides, too!

I drew a pentagon!

Draw a polygon with 4 sides that are the same length.

My next polygon will have 4 sides. A polygon with 4 sides is called a quadrilateral!

I drew a special kind of quadrilateral, called a rhombus. A rhombus has 4 sides that are all the same length.

Convince Me! Draw a quadrilateral with 4 sides that are the same length and with 4 right angles. Write 2 names for the quadrilateral.

☆ **Guided Practice** ☆ Draw each shape. Complete the sentences.

1. Draw a polygon with 3 vertices.

The polygon also has ___ sides.

The polygon is a

_____.

2. Draw a polygon with 6 sides.

The polygon also has ___ angles.

The polygon is a

_____.

© Pearson Education, Inc. 2
Topic 13 | Lesson 3

Name _____

Independent Practice ☆   Draw each shape. Complete the sentences.

3. Draw a polygon with
3 vertices and
1 right angle.

The polygon also has

_____ sides.

The polygon is

a _____.

4. Draw a quadrilateral with
opposite sides that are
the same length.

The polygon also has

_____ vertices.

The polygon is

a _____.

5. Draw a polygon with
4 sides that are
the same length.

The polygon also has

_____ angles.

The polygon is

a _____.

6. Draw a polygon with
4 sides that are
different lengths.

The polygon also has

_____ angles.

The polygon is

a _____.

7. Draw a polygon with
5 vertices and 3 sides
that are the same length.

The polygon also has

_____ sides in all.

The polygon is

a _____.

8. Higher Order Thinking
Can you draw a polygon
with 3 vertices and
4 sides? Explain.

9. Be Precise Draw a rectangle with 4 equal sides.

What is another name for this shape?

_____

10. Draw 3 shapes. The first shape is a quadrilateral. The number of vertices in each shape increases by one.

Name the third shape. _____

11. Higher Order Thinking The owner of Joe's Fish Market wants a new sign. He wants the sign to have curved sides. Draw a sign for Joe's Fish Market.

Is the sign a polygon? Explain.

_____

_____

12. 🚩 **Assessment Practice** David drew two different polygons. One of the polygons was a square. If David drew 9 sides and 9 vertices in all, what other polygon did David draw? 🚩 2.G.1.1

Ⓐ

Ⓑ

Ⓒ

Ⓓ

© Pearson Education, Inc. 2

Name _____

Solve & Share

Describe the two shapes in 4 or more ways. Tell how they are different and how they are the same. Use a tool to include measurements in your description.

I can …
draw cubes and describe how they look.

MAFS.2.G.1.1 Recognize and draw shapes having specified attributes, such as a given number of angles or a given number of equal faces. Identify triangles, quadrilaterals, pentagons, hexagons, and cubes. Also 2.MD.1.1
MAFS.K12.MP.2.1, MP.6.1, MP.7.1

A **cube** is a solid figure with 6 equal **faces**, 12 **edges**, and 8 vertices.

face → ← edge
← vertex

Each face is a square, with 4 equal edges and 4 right angles.

These are cubes.

These are **NOT** cubes.

You can use dot paper to draw a cube. The dashed lines show the edges that you can't see when you look at a solid cube.

Trace around each face.

Convince Me! What solid figure has 6 equal faces?

_____

What is the shape of each face?

_____

☆ **Guided Practice** ☆ Circle the cubes in the group of shapes. Be ready to explain how you know they are cubes.

1.

2. Use the dot paper. Draw a cube.

You can use the cube you traced as an example.

© Pearson Education, Inc. 2

Name _____

Independent Practice

Decide if the shape is a cube. Then draw a line from each shape to *cube* or **NOT** *a cube.*

3.

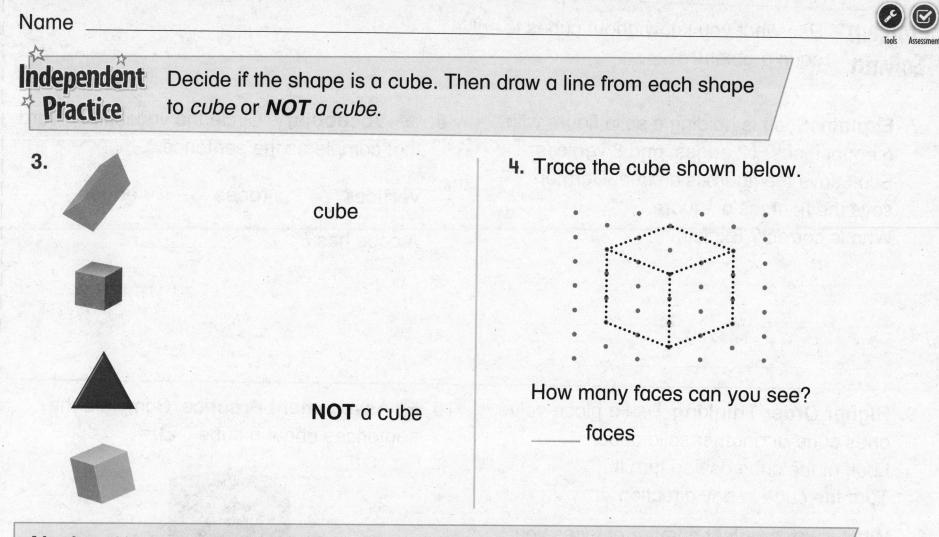

cube

NOT a cube

4. Trace the cube shown below.

How many faces can you see?

_____ faces

Algebra Use what you know about cubes to write an equation and solve each problem.

5. How many vertices do these two cubes have in all?

_____ + _____ = _____

_____ vertices

6. How many faces do these two cubes have in all?

_____ + _____ = _____

_____ faces

Topic 13 | Lesson 4

7. **Explain** Scott is holding a solid figure with 6 equal faces, 12 edges, and 8 vertices. Scott says the figure is a cube. Carmen says the figure is a square. Who is correct? Explain.

_____

_____

_____

8. **A-Z Vocabulary** Circle the vocabulary word that completes the sentence.

vertices   faces   edges

A cube has 6 _____.

9. **Higher Order Thinking** Use a place-value ones cube or another solid cube. Look at the cube as you turn it. Turn the cube in any direction.

What is the greatest number of faces you can see at one time? Explain.

_____

_____

_____

10. **Assessment Practice** Complete the sentences about a cube. 2.G.1.1

A cube is a solid _____.

A cube has _____ equal faces,

_____ vertices, and _____ edges.

© Pearson Education, Inc. 2

Name _____

Solve & Share

How many equal squares cover this rectangle? How could you show this with an addition equation?

I can ...
cover rectangles with equal-size squares and count to find the total number of them.

MAFS.2.G.1.2 Partition a rectangle into rows and columns of same-size squares and count to find the total number of them. **Also 2.OA.3.4** MAFS.K12.MP.3.1, MP.5.1, MP.7.1

Columns

Rows

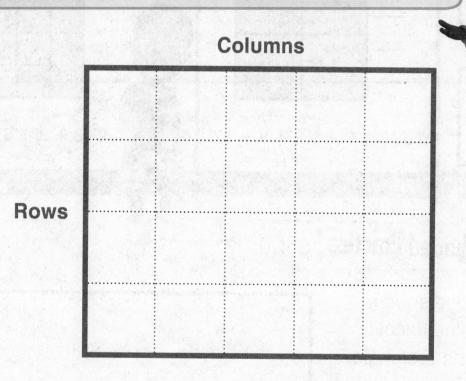

_____ equal squares

Equation: _____

Visual Learning   A-Z Glossary

How many red squares can cover this rectangle?

Begin like this:

NOT like this:

Count. Each row has 4 squares. You can add the squares by rows.

→
→
→

4 + 4 + 4 = 12

Count. Each column has 3 squares. You can add the squares by columns.

↓   ↓   ↓   ↓

3 + 3 + 3 + 3 = 12

Convince Me! Explain how you can cover a rectangle with equal-sized squares to help you find the total number of them.

☆ **Guided Practice** Solve.

1. Use square tiles to cover the rectangle. Trace the tiles. Column 1 is done for you.

2. Count and add. How many squares cover the rectangle?

   Add by rows: _____ + _____ + _____ = _____

   Add by columns:

   _____ + _____ + _____ + _____ + _____ + _____ = _____

© Pearson Education, Inc. 2

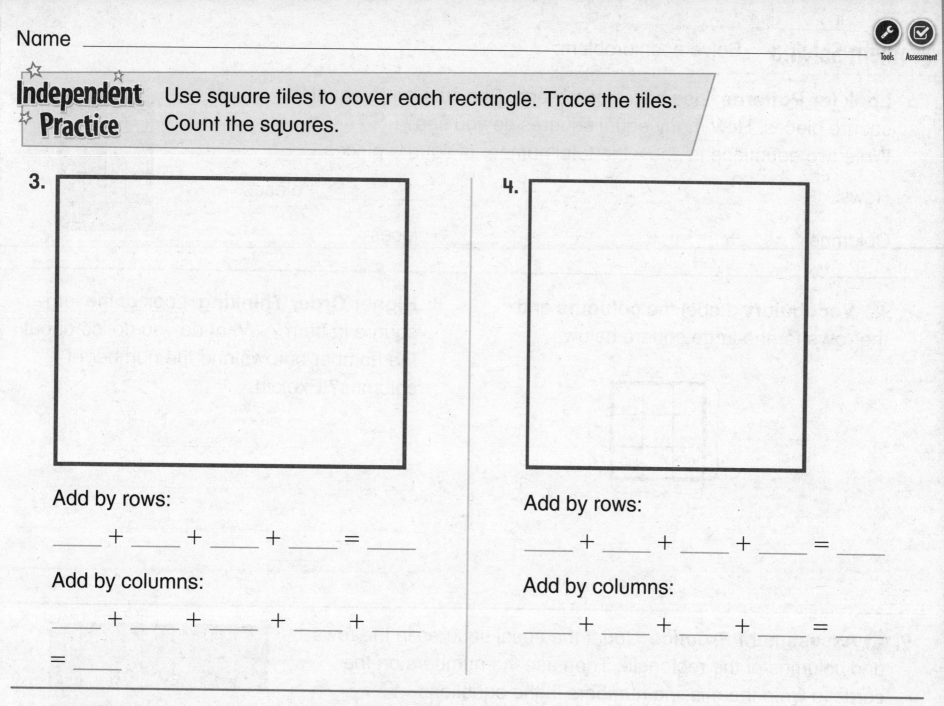

Name _____

Independent Practice

Use square tiles to cover each rectangle. Trace the tiles. Count the squares.

3.

Add by rows:

____ + ____ + ____ + ____ = ____

Add by columns:

____ + ____ + ____ + ____

= ____

4.

Add by rows:

____ + ____ + ____ + ____ = ____

Add by columns:

____ + ____ + ____ + ____ = ____

5. **Number Sense** Draw a rectangle that is made up of 6 equal squares.

Problem Solving ⭐ Solve each problem.

6. Look for Patterns Lisa bakes cornbread. She cuts it into equal square pieces. How many equal squares do you see?
Write two equations to show the total number of square pieces.

Rows: _____ + _____ + _____ + _____ + _____ + _____ = _____ pieces

Columns: _____ + _____ + _____ + _____ = _____ pieces

---

7. (A-Z) **Vocabulary** Label the **columns** and the **rows** for the large square below.

8. Higher Order Thinking Look at the large square in Item 7. What do you notice about the number of rows and the number of columns? Explain.

_____

_____

_____

_____

---

9. 🏴 **Assessment Practice** Count the equal squares in the rows and columns of the rectangle. Then use the numbers on the cards to write the missing numbers in the equations. 🏴 2.G.1.2

14	2	7

Rows: _____ + _____ = _____

Columns: _____ + _____ + _____ + _____ + _____ + _____ + _____ = _____

© Pearson Education, Inc. 2

Solve & Share

Fold a paper square one time to make equal shares. How many equal shares are there?

Fold a different square 2 times to make equal shares. How many equal shares are there?

Draw your fold lines on the squares below. What can you say about the number of folds and the number of equal shares?

I can ...
show circles and rectangles in halves, thirds, and fourths.

MAFS.2.G.1.3 Partition circles and rectangles into two, three, or four equal shares, describe the shares using the words *halves, thirds, half of, a third of,* etc., and describe the whole as two halves, three thirds, four fourths. Recognize that equal shares of identical wholes need not have the same shape. **Also 2.MD.1.2**
MAFS.K12.MP.2.1, MP.4.1, MP.6.1

1 Fold	2 Folds

_____ equal shares   _____ equal shares

Are these shares equal?

2 **equal shares**

These shares are **halves**.

NOT equal shares

These shares are not halves.

Are these shares equal?

3 equal shares

These shares are **thirds**.

NOT equal shares

These shares are not thirds.

Are these shares equal?

4 equal shares

These shares are **fourths**.

NOT equal shares

These shares are not fourths.

You can show equal shares in different ways.

Each share is a fourth of the whole.

Convince Me! Show this rectangle with three equal shares. How many thirds is one share? How many thirds is the whole rectangle?

☆ **Guided Practice** Solve each problem.

1. Show each square in halves. Show four different ways.

2. Tell what part of the whole each equal share is. Write *a half of, a third of,* or *a fourth of*.

© Pearson Education, Inc. 2

Topic 13 | Lesson 6

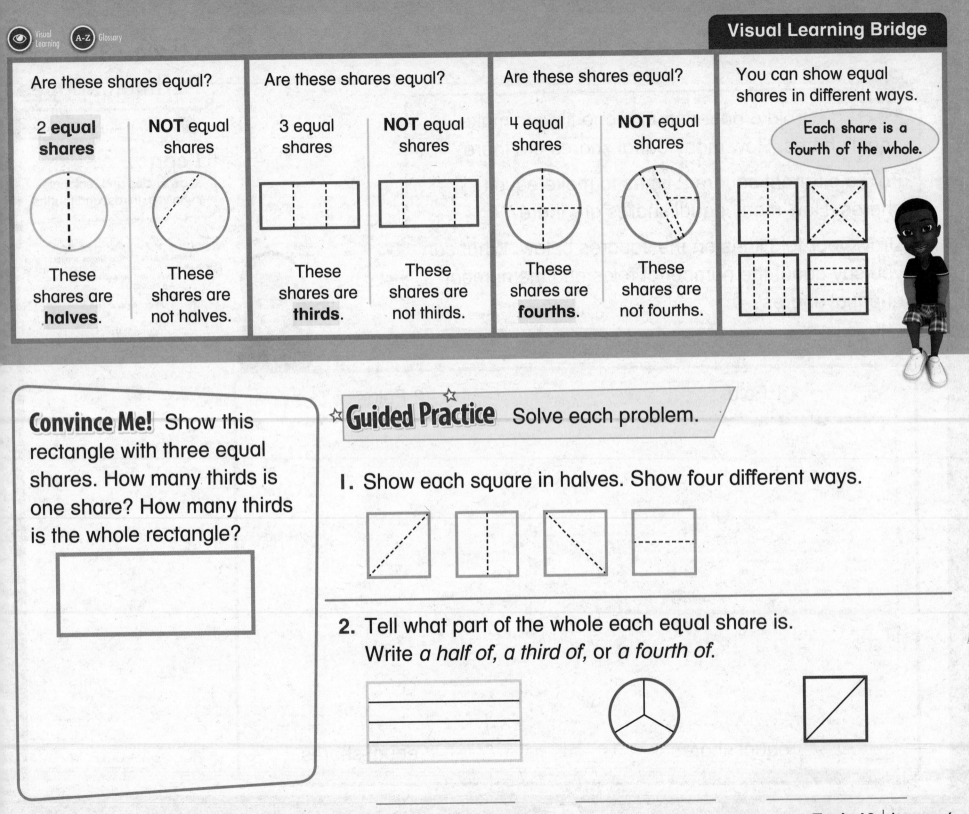

Independent Practice

Show each shape with the number of equal shares given. Show 2 ways. Then complete the sentences.

3. 3 equal shares

Each share is _____ the whole.

Each whole is _____.

4. 4 equal shares

Each share is _____ the whole.

Each whole is _____.

5. 2 equal shares

Each share is _____ the whole.

Each whole is _____.

6. Higher Order Thinking Draw what comes next.

7. Model Leon cut a waffle into halves. Draw lines to show 3 different ways he could have cut the waffle.

8. enVision® STEM Tina is planting a garden. She wants to have equal parts for beans, for tomatoes, and for peppers. Draw a picture of how she could plant her garden.

9. Higher Order Thinking Draw lines on the picture to solve the problem.

4 friends want to share a watermelon. How could they cut the watermelon so each friend gets an equal share?

Each friend will get _____.

10. 🐦 **Assessment Practice** Matt wants a flag that shows fourths. Which flags could Matt use? Choose all that apply. 🐦 2.G.1.3

Activity

Solve & Share

Use a crayon to show 4 equal shares of this pizza. Compare your answer with a partner. Did you both make 4 equal shares? Do your shares look the same?

I can ...

make equal shares that do not have the same shape.

MAFS.2.G.1.3 Partition circles and rectangles into two, three, or four equal shares, describe the shares using the words *halves, thirds, half of, a third of*, etc., and describe the whole as two halves, three thirds, four fourths. Recognize that equal shares of identical wholes need not have the same shape. **Also 2.OA.3.4**
MAFS.K12.MP.2.1, MP.3.1

How can this square be shown with 3 equal shares?

You can use the smaller squares to help.

These show equal shares that are all the same shape.

You can draw lines to make 3 columns or 3 rows.

This shows equal shares that are **NOT** all the same shape.

Each share is 3 squares. The shares are equal.

Each way shows 3 equal shares.

Equal shares can be different shapes.

Convince Me! How can you check to make sure all of the shares are equal?

☆ **Guided Practice** ☆ Draw lines to show 2 equal shares. Each way should be different.

1.

2. How many squares are in each equal share of the rectangles?

_____

3. Describe the equal shares and the whole.

Each share is _a half of_ the whole.

Each whole is _two halves_.

© Pearson Education, Inc. 2

Name _____

⭐ Independent ⭐ Practice

Draw lines in each rectangle to show 4 equal shares. Each way should be different. Then answer the questions.

4. Show equal shares that are the **same shape**.

Show equal shares that are **different shapes**.

5. How many squares are in each equal share in Item 4? _____

6. Describe the equal shares and the whole in Item 4.

Each share is _____ the whole.

Each whole is _____.

Draw lines to show 3 equal shares in two different ways.

7.

8. Higher Order Thinking How can equal shares in a rectangle have different shapes?

_____

_____

_____

9. Allen wants to share this pan of corn bread with 3 friends. Allen and his friends will each get an equal share.

How many pieces will be in each share?

_____ pieces

10. **Explain** Greg says that equal shares can be different in shape and size. Is Greg correct? Explain.

_____

_____

_____

11. **Higher Order Thinking** Donna drew the line in this rectangle to make 2 equal shares. Are the shares equal? Why or why not?

_____

_____

12. 🔘 **Assessment Practice** Meg shows a rectangle with 3 equal shares that are **NOT** the same shape. Which could be Meg's rectangle? 2.G.1.3

Ⓐ   Ⓒ

Ⓑ   Ⓓ

© Pearson Education, Inc. 2

Topic 13 | Lesson 7

Name _____

★ **Solve & Share**

Design two different flags. Draw 15 equal-size squares in each flag. Use rows and columns.

Make three equal shares of different colors in each flag. Then write an equation for each flag to show the total number of squares.

I can ...
use repeated reasoning to show rectangles with rows and columns and create designs with equal shares.

MAFS.K12.MP.8.1 Look for and express regularity in repeated reasoning. **Also** MP.1.1, MP.2.1, MP.3.1, MP.4.1, MP.7.1 MAFS.2.G.1.2 Partition a rectangle into rows and columns of same-size squares and count to find the total number of them. **Also 2.G.1.3, 2.OA.3.4**

My Flag Designs

Equation:

_____

Equation:

_____

Thinking Habits

Does something repeat in the problem?

How can the solution help me solve another problem?

Sam is designing a square quilt. The quilt must have 4 colors with an equal share for each color.

Help Sam make two designs.

How can I look for things that repeat in the problem?

Each share has 4 small squares. So, any shape with 4 small squares is an equal share.

I can make shares that are the same shape. These fourths are all squares.

Design 1

In both designs, the fourths are equal in size.

Here, I used different shapes for the shares.

Design 2

Convince Me! How do you know each share in Design 2 is a fourth of the whole square?

☆**Guided Practice**☆   Solve the problem. Use crayons to color.

1. Hamal is painting a design. The design must have 3 colors with an equal share for each color. Create two possible designs for Hamal.

Design 1   **Design 2**

Be ready to explain how you used repeated reasoning to help you solve the problem.

© Pearson Education, Inc. 2

Independent Practice ✦ Solve each problem. Use crayons to color. Explain your work.

2. Marie wants to put a rectangular design on a T-shirt. The design must have 4 colors with an equal share for each color. Create two possible designs for Marie.

Design 1   **Design 2**

_____

_____

_____

_____

3. Grant wants to put a circle design on his toy car. The design must have 3 colors with an equal share for each color. Create two possible designs for Grant.

Design 1   **Design 2**

_____

_____

_____

_____

Problem Solving

Tile Design

Ms. Walton created this rectangular tile design. What share of the design is orange? What share of the design is yellow? How many shares is the whole design? How many thirds is the whole?

4. **Make Sense** How does Ms. Walton's design show equal shares? Explain.

2.G.I.3, MP.I.I

_____

_____

_____

_____

5. **Reasoning** What share of the design is orange? What share of the design is yellow? How many shares is the whole design? How many thirds is the whole? 2.G.I.3, MP.2.I

_____

_____

_____

_____

6. **Generalize** Copy the tile design above onto this grid. Then color it orange and yellow to match the design shown above.

How did you copy the design? Describe one or two shortcuts you used.

MP.8.I

_____

_____

© Pearson Education, Inc. 2

Follow the Path

Find each sum or difference. Then color a path from **Start** to **Finish**. Follow the sums and differences that are even numbers. You can only move up, down, right, or left.

I can ...
add and subtract within 100.

MAFS.2.NBT.2.5

Start								
69 − 23	31 + 25	78 − 47	97 − 49	72 + 12	76 − 38	67 − 47	48 + 24	46 + 37
84 − 61	73 − 55	68 + 29	11 + 17	37 + 58	86 − 51	21 + 38	82 − 18	81 − 62
43 + 42	27 + 49	35 + 48	46 − 32	73 − 26	30 + 31	46 − 28	47 + 41	62 − 39
25 + 16	60 − 36	50 − 29	39 + 43	60 − 45	64 + 23	29 + 35	56 + 41	94 − 61
35 + 42	85 − 23	24 + 56	58 + 36	97 − 38	25 − 16	38 + 62	79 − 49	59 + 23
								Finish

Understand Vocabulary

Write *always*, *sometimes*, or *never*.

Word List

• angle	• hexagon
• cube	• pentagon
• edge	• polygon
• equal shares	• quadrilateral
• face	• right angle
• fourths	• thirds
• halves	• vertex

1. A cube has exactly 4 faces. _____

2. A right angle forms a square corner. _____

3. Quadrilaterals are squares. _____

4. A solid figure with faces has edges. _____

Draw a line from each term to its example.

5. hexagon   **6.** pentagon   **7.** vertex

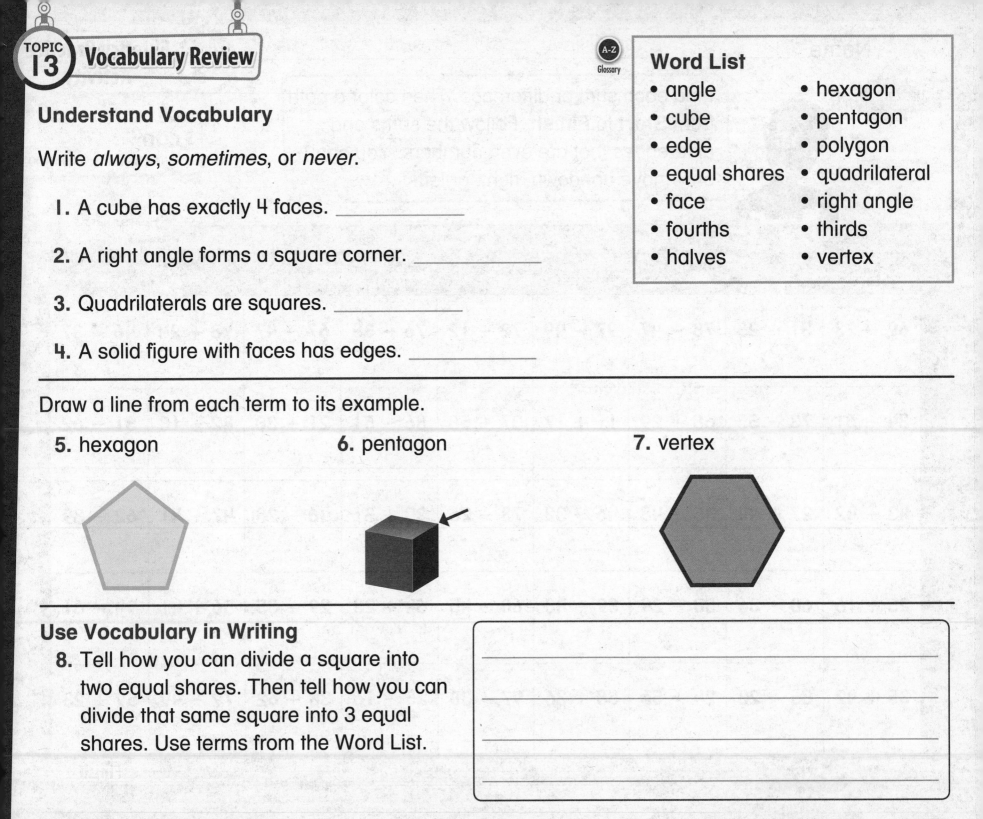

Use Vocabulary in Writing

8. Tell how you can divide a square into two equal shares. Then tell how you can divide that same square into 3 equal shares. Use terms from the Word List.

Name _____

Set A

You can name a plane shape by its number of sides and vertices.

vertex

side

__3__ sides

__3__ vertices

Shape: _triangle_

__4__ sides

__4__ vertices

Shape:

quadrilateral

Write the number of sides and vertices. Name the shape.

1. ____ sides

____ vertices

Shape: _____

2. ____ sides

____ vertices

Shape: _____

Set B

You can name a polygon by the number of its angles.

__5__ angles

pentagon

__6__ angles

hexagon

Write the number of angles. Then name the shape.

3.

____ angles

Shape: _____

4.

____ angles

Shape: _____

You can draw a polygon with a given number of sides, vertices, or angles.

Draw a polygon with 4 sides. Two sides have different lengths.

Draw a polygon with 5 vertices.

Draw a polygon with 3 angles. One angle is a right angle.

Draw each polygon described.

5. 6 sides

6. 3 vertices

7. 5 sides and 2 right angles

8. 8 angles

Set D

You can describe and draw cubes.

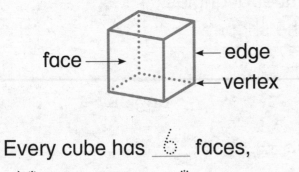

face → ← edge

← vertex

Every cube has __6__ faces,

__12__ edges, and __8__ vertices.

9. Cross out the shapes that are **NOT** cubes.

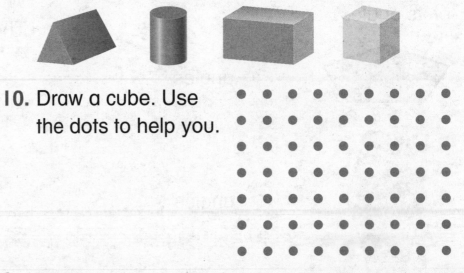

10. Draw a cube. Use the dots to help you.

© Pearson Education, Inc. 2

Name _____

Set E

You can cover a rectangle with squares.

column

row →

Count by rows: $3 + 3 = 6$

Count by columns: $2 + 2 + 2 = 6$

_6_ squares cover the rectangle.

Use square tiles to cover the rectangle. Trace the tiles. Then count the squares.

11.

_____ squares cover the rectangle.

Set F

You can show circles and rectangles with equal shares.

2 equal shares are **halves**.

3 equal shares are **thirds**.

4 equal shares are **fourths**.

Show each shape with the given number of equal shares. Show 2 ways.

12. halves

13. thirds

14. fourths

Equal shares can be different shapes.

This is one way to show this rectangle

with __3__ equal shares.

Each equal share is __4__ squares.

Draw lines to show 2 more ways these rectangles can have 3 equal shares.

15. equal shares that are **NOT** all the same shape

16. equal shares that are all the same shape

Thinking Habits

Repeated Reasoning

Does something repeat in the problem?

How can the solution help me solve another problem?

Use the design shown. Create a different design with 3 equal shares.

17.

© Pearson Education, Inc. 2

Topic 13 | Reteaching

Name _____

1. Which polygons are pentagons?

2. Rita draws a polygon. It has fewer than 8 sides and more angles than a square. Which shape did Rita draw?

Ⓐ triangle

Ⓑ rectangle

Ⓒ hexagon

Ⓓ quadrilateral

3. Which rectangles are shown in fourths? Choose all that apply.

4. Draw a polygon with 4 angles.
   Make one angle a right angle.
   Then name the polygon.

Name: _____

5. Is the polygon a quadrilateral? Choose Yes or No.

I have 3 sides and 3 angles. ○ Yes ○ No

I have 4 sides and 4 angles. ○ Yes ○ No

I am a square. ○ Yes ○ No

I am a rectangle. ○ Yes ○ No

6. Mandy draws a polygon with 6 sides and 6 angles. Which shape did she draw?

Ⓐ pentagon

Ⓑ hexagon

Ⓒ octagon

Ⓓ quadrilateral

7. Name the shape below. Write 3 things that describe the shape.

8. Draw the polygon described below. Then complete the sentence.

I have 2 fewer sides than a pentagon.
I have 1 less angle than a square.
I have one right angle.

The shape is a _____.

9. Complete the sentence to name and describe the solid figure below.

A _____ has ____ faces, ____ vertices, and ____ edges.

10. Show this circle with 2 equal shares. Then complete the sentences.

Each share is a _____ of the whole.

The whole is ____ halves.

11. Brad says there are only two ways to divide the same rectangle below into 3 equal shares. Do you agree? Use words and pictures to explain.

_____

_____

12. Count the number of squares in the rows and columns of the rectangle. Use the numbers on the cards to write the missing numbers in the equations.

| 15 | 3 | 5 |

Rows: ____ + ____ + ____ = ____ squares

Columns: ____ + ____ + ____ + ____ + ____ = ____ squares

13. Kerry wants a design that shows thirds. Which designs could Kerry use? Choose all that apply.

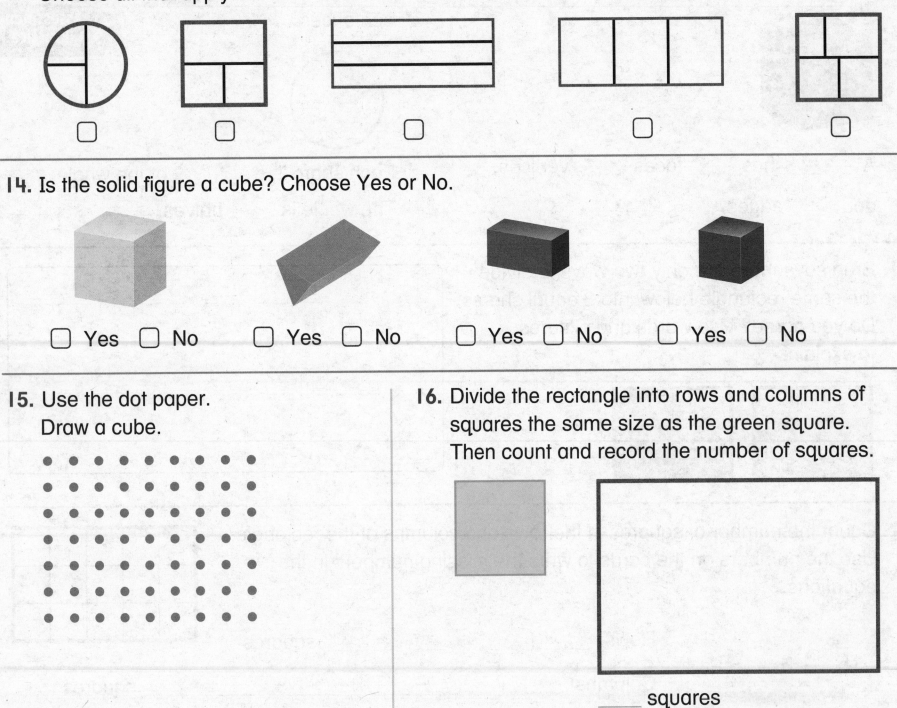

☐   ☐   ☐   ☐   ☐

14. Is the solid figure a cube? Choose Yes or No.

☐ Yes ☐ No   ☐ Yes ☐ No   ☐ Yes ☐ No   ☐ Yes ☐ No

15. Use the dot paper. Draw a cube.

16. Divide the rectangle into rows and columns of squares the same size as the green square. Then count and record the number of squares.

_____ squares

Name _____

Happy Home

Tina and her family moved into a new home.
They bought different things for each room.

1. They hang pictures on the wall.
   Name the shape of each picture frame.

    2.G.1.1

_____

_____

2. The rug in the kitchen has
   5 sides and 5 vertices.
   Draw the shape of the rug.

   2.G.1.1, MP.1.1

   Name the shape. _____

3. The wallpaper uses this pattern.

   2.G.1.1, MP.3.1

   Name the shape in the pattern.

   _____

   Write the number of sides, vertices, and
   angles in the shape.

   _____ sides   _____ vertices   _____ angles

4. The living room has 2 end tables.

2.G.1.1, MP.3.1

Circle the table that is a cube. Explain.

_____

_____

_____

_____

5. Tina has a new quilt for her bed. Her quilt has this design.   2.G.1.3

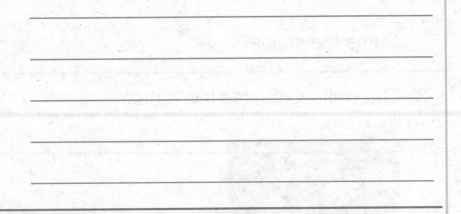

What share is green? _____

What share is yellow? _____

6. Tina's mother is making a quilt with smaller squares. She wants the quilt to have 4 colors. Each color has an equal share.

2.G.1.2, 2.G.1.3, MP.8.1

Part A

Use 4 colors to make a quilt design below. Make the equal shares the same shape.

Design I

Part B

Use 4 colors to make a different quilt design below. Make equal shares that are not all the same shape.

Design 2

© Pearson Education, Inc. 2

Topic 13 | Performance Task

More Addition, Subtraction, and Length

Essential Question: How can you add and subtract lengths?

Look at the big waves! Look at the big rock!

Water and land in an area can have different sizes and shapes.

Wow! Let's do this project and learn more.

Digital Resources

Interactive Student Edition · Activity · Visual Learning · Video · Practice

Assessment · Games · Tools · Glossary

MAFS.2.OA.1.1, 2.MD.2.5, 2.MD.2.6
MAFS.K12.MP.1.1, MP.2.1, MP.3.1, MP.4.1, MP.5.1, MP.6.1, MP.7.1, MP.8.1

enVision STEM Project: Modeling Land, Water, and Length

Find Out Find and share books and other sources that show the shapes and kinds of land and water in an area. Draw a picture or make a model to show the land or water in an area.

Journal: Make a Book Show what you learn in a book. In your book, also:

• Draw a picture to show the shape of some land or water in your area.

• Make up a math story about lengths. Draw a picture to show how to solve the problem in your story.

Name _____

Review What You Know

Vocabulary

1. Circle the measuring unit that is better to **estimate** the **length** of a room.

meter

centimeter

2. Circle the number of feet in 1 **yard**.

2 feet

3 feet

4 feet

12 feet

3. The clock shows the time a math class begins. Circle **a.m.** or **p.m.**

a.m.

p.m.

Estimate

4. Estimate the length of the eraser in centimeters.

About _____ centimeters

Compare

5. A sidewalk is 632 yards long. A jogging trail is 640 yards long.

Use <, >, or = to compare the lengths.

632 ◯ 640

Rectangles

6. Label the 2 missing lengths of the sides of the rectangle.

4 cm

_____ cm

3 cm

_____ cm

© Pearson Education, Inc. 2

Name _____

How tall are Ferris wheels?

Project: Write a Ferris Wheel Story

How big are insects?

Project: Make Insect Models

PROJECT
14C

How can you measure if you do not have tools?

Project: Make a Measurement Poster

PROJECT
14D

How is some food grown?

Project: Draw a Garden Plan

© Pearson Education, Inc. 2

Topic 14 | Pick a Project

Name _____

Solve & Share

The ant crawled along the edge of this blue rectangle. Measure the total distance the ant crawled. Show your work and be ready to explain it.

I can ...

solve problems by adding or subtracting length measurements.

MAFS.2.MD.2.5 Use addition and subtraction within 100 to solve word problems involving lengths that are given in the same units, e.g., by using drawings (such as drawings of rulers) and equations with a symbol for the unknown number to represent the problem. **Also 2.OA.1.1**
MAFS.K12.MP.2.1, MP.4.1, MP.6.1

Visual Learning   A-Z Glossary

The book is 9 inches long and 6 inches wide.

What is the distance around the front cover of the book?

6 in.

Front Cover   9 in.

Add the lengths of all four sides to find the distance around the cover.

$9 + 6 + 9 + 6 = ?$

$18 + 12 =$

$10 + 10 + 8 + 2 =$

$20 + 10 = 30$

The distance around the cover is 30 inches.

Think: Will I add or subtract?

How much longer is the teacher's arm than the child's arm?

Arm Length in Centimeters

Teacher	66
Child	47

Subtract to compare measurements.

$66 - 47 = ?$

40   7

6   1

$66 - 40 = 26$

$26 - 6 = 20$

$20 - 1 = 19$

The teacher's arm is 19 centimeters longer than the child's arm.

Convince Me! Explain how to find the distance around a square park that is 2 miles long on each side.

Guided Practice Decide if you need to add or subtract.
Then write an equation to help solve each problem.

1. What is the distance around the baseball card?

   $10 + 7 + 10 + 7 = 34$

   Distance around: ___34___ cm

   10 cm

   7 cm

2. What is the distance around the puzzle?

   _____

   Distance around: _____ in.

   15 in.

   12 in.

Tools   Assessment

Independent Practice   Decide if you need to add or subtract.
Then write an equation to help solve each problem.

3. What is the distance around the door?

3 ft

7 ft

_____

Distance around: _____ ft

---

4. What is the distance around the cell phone?

2 in.

4 in.

_____

Distance around: _____ in.

---

5. How much longer is the red scarf than the blue scarf?

60 in.

45 in.

_____

_____ in. longer

---

6. **Algebra** What is the length of the shorter side of the rectangle? Complete the equation to solve.

20 cm

?

$20 + \underline{\hspace{1cm}} + 20 + \underline{\hspace{1cm}} = 60$

The shorter side is _____ centimeters.

An equation is a model.

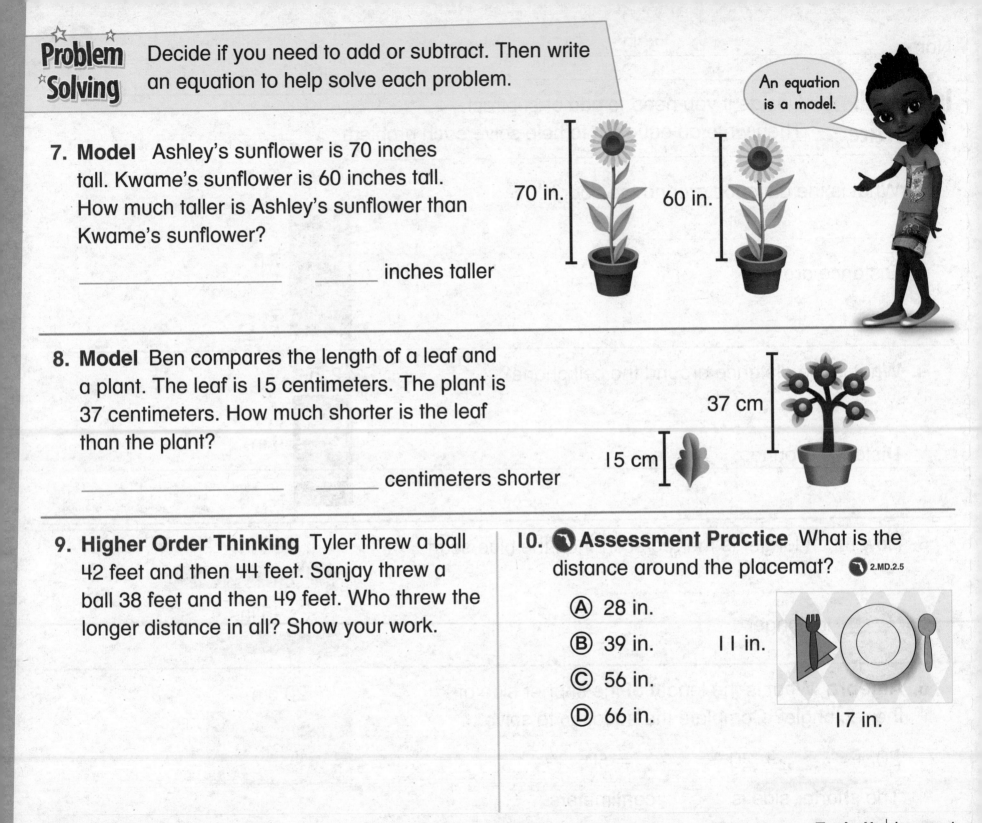

7. **Model** Ashley's sunflower is 70 inches tall. Kwame's sunflower is 60 inches tall. How much taller is Ashley's sunflower than Kwame's sunflower?

70 in.   60 in.

_____ _____ inches taller

8. **Model** Ben compares the length of a leaf and a plant. The leaf is 15 centimeters. The plant is 37 centimeters. How much shorter is the leaf than the plant?

37 cm

15 cm

_____ _____ centimeters shorter

9. **Higher Order Thinking** Tyler threw a ball 42 feet and then 44 feet. Sanjay threw a ball 38 feet and then 49 feet. Who threw the longer distance in all? Show your work.

10. **Assessment Practice** What is the distance around the placemat? 2.MD.2.5

Ⓐ 28 in.
Ⓑ 39 in.   11 in.
Ⓒ 56 in.
Ⓓ 66 in.

17 in.

© Pearson Education, Inc. 2
Topic 14 | Lesson 1

Solve & Share

Julie and Steve each cut a piece of yarn.
The total length of both pieces is 12 cm.

Measure each piece of yarn.
Circle Julie and Steve's pieces. Then explain your thinking.

Activity

Lesson 14-2

Find Unknown Measurements

I can ...
add or subtract to solve problems about measurements.

MAFS.2.MD.2.5 Use addition and subtraction within 100 to solve word problems involving lengths that are given in the same units, e.g., by using drawings (such as drawings of rulers) and equations with a symbol for the unknown number to represent the problem. Also 2.OA.1.1
MAFS.K12.MP.1.1, MP.3.1, MP.4.1

_____
_____
_____

Michelle jumped 24 inches. Tim jumped 7 fewer inches than Michelle. How far did Tim jump?

What operation should I use?

You can write a subtraction equation to show the problem.

The length of Tim's jump is unknown.

24 — 7 = ?

length of Michelle's jump   fewer inches   length of Tim's jump

You can draw a picture, such as a yardstick. Then count back to solve the problem.

− 7 in.

Tim jumped 17 inches.

Convince Me! How does drawing a yardstick help you solve the problem above?

☆ **Guided Practice** ☆ Write an equation using a ? for the unknown number. Solve with a picture or another way.

1. A square stamp measures 2 centimeters in length. How many centimeters long are two stamps?

2 + 2 = ?

1 cm 1 cm 1 cm 1 cm = 4 cm

_____ cm

2. Stuart's desk is 64 centimeters long. His dresser is 7 centimeters longer than his desk. How long is Stuart's dresser?

_____ _____ cm

© Pearson Education, Inc. 2
Topic 14 | Lesson 2

Name _____

Independent Practice Write an equation using a ? for the unknown number. Solve with a picture or another way.

3. Filipe's pencil box is 24 centimeters long. Joe's pencil box is 3 centimeters shorter than Filipe's. How long is Joe's pencil box?

_____   _____ cm

4. Clark threw a red ball and a blue ball. He threw the red ball 17 feet. He threw the blue ball 7 feet farther. How far did Clark throw the blue ball?

_____   _____ ft

5. **enVision®** STEM Ashlie's map shows where animals, land, and water are at a zoo.

The distance around her map is 38 inches. What is the length of the missing side?

8 in.

11 in.   ? in.

8 in.

_____

_____ inches

6. Make Sense A brown puppy is 43 centimeters tall. A spotted puppy is 7 centimeters shorter than the brown puppy. A white puppy is 14 centimeters taller than the brown puppy. How tall is the spotted puppy? Think about what you need to find.

_____ cm

7. 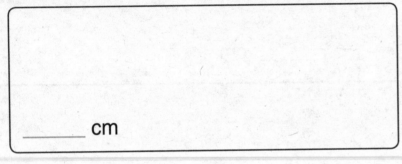 **Vocabulary** Complete the sentences using the terms below.

foot   **yard**   **inch**

A paper clip is about 1 _____ long.

My math book is about 1 _____ long.

A baseball bat is about 1 _____ long.

8. Higher Order Thinking Jack jumped 15 inches. Tyler jumped 1 inch less than Jack and 2 inches more than Randy. Who jumped the farthest? How far did each person jump?

9. **Assessment Practice** Kim was 48 inches tall in January. She grew 9 inches during the year. How tall is Kim at the end of the year? Write an equation with an unknown and then draw a picture to solve.   2.MD.2.5

_____

_____ in.

Name _____

Solve & Share

Alex has a piece of ribbon that is 45 feet long. He cuts the ribbon. Now he has 39 feet of ribbon. How many feet of ribbon did Alex cut off?

Draw a picture and write an equation to solve. Show your work.

I can ...

add and subtract to solve measurement problems by using drawings and equations.

MAFS.2.MD.2.5 Use addition and subtraction within 100 to solve word problems involving lengths that are given in the same units, e.g., by using drawings (such as drawings of rulers) and equations with a symbol for the unknown number to represent the problem. **Also 2.OA.1.1** **MAFS.K12.MP.1.1, MP.3.1, MP.7.1**

A string is 28 cm.
Alex cuts off a piece.
Now the string is 16 cm.
How long is the piece of
string Alex cut off?

You can write an addition
or subtraction equation.

$$28 - ? = 16$$

length at first — length cut — length now

$$16 + ? = 28$$

length now — length cut — length at first

You can draw a picture for $28 - ? = 16$ or $16 + ? = 28$.

– 2 cm — – 10 cm

15 16 17 18 19 20 21 22 23 24 25 26 27 28

$$28 - \underline{12} = 16$$

+ 4 cm — + 8 cm

15 16 17 18 19 20 21 22 23 24 25 26 27 28

$$16 + \underline{12} = 28$$

Alex cut off 12 cm of string.

Convince Me! How does
writing an equation help you
solve the problem above?

✰ **Guided Practice** ✰ Write an equation using a ? for the unknown
number. Solve with a picture or another way.

1. A plant was 15 inches tall.
It grew and is now 22 inches
tall. How many inches did the
plant grow?

+ 5 in. — + 2 in.

14 15 16 17 18 19 20 21 22 23

$$15 + ? = 22$$

2. Each bus is 10 meters long.
Each boat is 7 meters long.
What is the total length of two
buses and two boats?

© Pearson Education, Inc. 2

Topic 14 | Lesson 3

Name _____

★ Independent ★ Practice

Write an equation using a ? for the unknown number.
Solve with a picture or another way.

3. Brent's rope is 49 inches long. He cuts off
some of the rope and now it is 37 inches long.
How much rope did Brent cut off?

_____   _____

4. Sue ran for some meters and stopped. Then
she ran another 22 meters for a total of
61 meters in all. How many meters did she run
at first?

_____   _____

5. **Algebra** Solve each equation. Use the chart.

○	=	12
☆	=	39
△	=	42
☐	=	57

○ + ☆ = _____

☐ − ☆ = _____

☆ + △ + ○ = _____

6. Make Sense The yellow boat is 15 feet shorter than the green boat. The green boat is 53 feet long. How long is the yellow boat? Think about what you are trying to find.

Write an equation to solve. Show your work.

_____ ft

7. 🅰🅉 Vocabulary Steve measured the length of his desk. It measured 2 units.

Circle the unit Steve used.

meter   foot   centimeter   inch

Lori measured the length of her cat. It measured 45 units.

Circle the unit Lori used.

centimeter   yard   inch   foot

8. Higher Order Thinking Lucy's ribbon is 1 foot long. Kathleen's ribbon is 15 inches long. Whose ribbon is longer and by how many inches? Explain your thinking.

_____

_____

_____

9. 🅵 Assessment Practice Mary's water bottle is 25 cm long. Joey's water bottle is 22 cm long. Ella's water bottle is 17 cm long.

Which statements are correct? Choose all that apply. 🅣 2.MD.2.5

☐ Mary's bottle is 8 cm longer than Ella's.

☐ Joey's bottle is 6 cm longer than Ella's.

☐ Joey's bottle is 3 cm shorter than Mary's.

☐ Ella's bottle is 8 cm longer than Mary's.

Solve & Share

Amelia walks 18 blocks on Monday and 5 blocks on Tuesday. How many blocks does she walk in all?

Use the number line to show how many blocks Amelia walks. Then write an equation to show your work.

I can ...
add and subtract on a number line.

MAFS.2.MD.2.6 Represent whole numbers as lengths from 0 on a number line diagram with equally spaced points corresponding to the numbers 0, 1, 2, . . ., and represent whole-number sums and differences within 100 on a number line diagram. **Also 2.OA.1.1** MAFS.K12.MP.2.1, MP.3.1, MP.5.1

0   5   10   15   20   25   30

Visual Learning   A-Z Glossary

Amelia walks 17 blocks before dinner. She walks 8 blocks after dinner. How many blocks does she walk in all?

You can use a number line to add lengths.
First, show the 17 blocks Amelia walks before dinner.
Then, add the 8 blocks she walks after dinner.

Start at 0.

$17 + 8 = 25$ blocks in all

Amelia buys 17 feet of rope. She cuts off 8 feet of rope to make a jump rope. How many feet of rope does she have left?

You can also use a number line to subtract lengths.
First, show the 17 feet of rope.
Then, subtract the 8 feet of rope she cuts off.

$17 - 8 = 9$ feet of rope left

Convince Me! Explain how to add 14 inches and 11 inches using a number line.

☆ **Guided Practice**   Use the number lines to add or subtract.

1. $21 + 7 =$ ___28___

2. $28 - 14 =$ _____

© Pearson Education, Inc. 2

☆ Independent Practice ☆ Use the number lines to add or subtract.

3. $80 - 35 =$ _____

0 5 10 15 20 25 30 35 40 45 50 55 60 65 70 75 80 85 90 95 100

4. $19 + 63 =$ _____

0 5 10 15 20 25 30 35 40 45 50 55 60 65 70 75 80 85 90 95 100

5. Higher Order Thinking Use the number line to show 15 inches plus 0 inches. Explain your thinking.

0   5   10   15   20   25   30

_____

6. Number Sense Show each number below as a length from 0 on the number line. Draw four separate arrows.

9   14   24   28

0   5   10   15   20   25   30

7. Use Tools A football team gains 15 yards on its first play. The team gains 12 yards on its second play. How many yards does the team gain in two plays?

_____ yards

8. Use Tools Mia buys 25 feet of board. She uses 16 feet of board for a sandbox. How many feet of board does she have left?

A number line is a tool you can use to add and subtract.

_____ feet

9. Higher Order Thinking The runners on the track team ran 12 miles on Monday. On Tuesday, they ran 6 more miles than they ran on Monday. How many miles did they run in all on both days?

_____ miles

10. 🅕 **Assessment Practice** Deb has two pencils. One pencil is 9 cm long and the other pencil is 13 cm long. What is the total length of both pencils?

Use the number line to show your work.

🅕 2.MD.2.6

_____ centimeters

© Pearson Education, Inc. 2

Name _____

Solve & Share

Choose a tool to solve each part of the problem. Be ready to explain which tools you used and why.

Which line is longer? How much longer?
Draw a line that is that length.

I can ...
choose the best tool to use to solve problems.

MAFS.K12.MP.5.1 Use appropriate tools strategically. Also MP.1.1, MP.3.1, MP.4.1, MP.6.1, MP.8.1
MAFS.2.MD.2.5 Use addition and subtraction within 100 to solve word problems involving lengths that are given in the same units, e.g., by using drawings (such as drawings of rulers) and equations with a symbol for the unknown number to represent the problem.
Also 2.MD.2.6, 2.OA.1.1

Thinking Habits

Which of these tools can I use?

counters   paper and pencil
cubes   place-value blocks
measuring tools   string
number line   technology

Am I using the tool correctly?

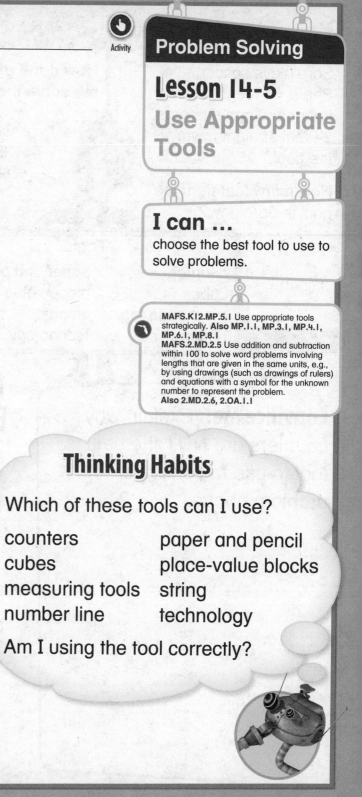

Sara plays soccer. She is 56 feet away from the goal. Then she runs 24 feet straight toward the goal.

How many feet from the goal is Sara now?

How can I use a tool to help me solve the problem?

I can think of tools that could help me. Then I can choose the best tool to use.

Tools

counters	paper and pencil
cubes	place-value blocks
measuring tools	string
number line	technology

I don't need a measuring tool. The units are given in feet. I need to subtract. I will draw a number line.

I can use paper and pencil to check my work.

$$56 - 24 = ?$$

– 24 feet

30 32 35   40   45   50   55 56   60

Sara is 32 feet from the goal.

$$\begin{array}{r} 56 \\ -20 \\ \hline 36 \\ -4 \\ \hline 32 \end{array}$$

Convince Me! Explain why counters are **NOT** the best tool to use to solve the problem above.

☆ **Guided Practice** ☆ Choose a tool to use to solve the problem. Show your work. Explain why you chose that tool and how you got your answer.

1. Sara cut 19 centimeters of ribbon into two pieces. One piece is 11 centimeters long. How long is the other piece?

© Pearson Education, Inc. 2

Independent Practice   Solve each problem. Show your work.

2. Work with a partner. Measure each other's arm from the shoulder to the tip of the index finger. Measure to the nearest inch. Whose arm is longer and by how much?

   Choose a tool to use to solve the problem. Explain why you chose that tool and how you got your answer.

3. Marcel jumped 39 centimeters high. Jamal jumped 48 centimeters high. How much higher did Jamal jump than Marcel?

   Which tool would you **NOT** use to solve this problem? Explain.

Problem Solving

Sailboats

Zak is measuring sailboats at the dock.

Mr. Lee's sailboat is 64 feet long.

Ms. Flint's sailboat is 25 feet shorter than Mr. Lee's boat.

Help Zak find the length of Ms. Flint's boat.

4. Use Tools Which tool would you **NOT** use to solve this problem? Explain. 🐾 MP.5.1

_____

_____

_____

5. Be Precise Will you add or subtract to solve the problem? 🐾 2.OA.1.1, 2.MD.2.5, MP.6.1

_____

Write an equation. Use ? for the unknown.

_____

What unit of measure will you use?

_____

6. Explain What is the length of Ms. Flint's boat? Did you use a tool to solve the problem? Explain. 🐾 2.OA.1.1, 2.MD.2.5, MP.3.1

_____

_____

Follow the Path

Color a path from **Start** to **Finish**. Follow the sums and differences that are odd numbers. You can only move up, down, right, or left.

Fluency Practice Activity

I can ...
add and subtract within 100.

MAFS.2.NBT.2.5

Start								
80 − 23	94 − 73	21 + 22	45 + 36	19 + 24	86 − 53	14 + 15	25 − 17	35 + 49
65 − 21	97 − 35	35 + 23	12 + 20	98 − 12	74 − 48	27 + 48	54 + 46	53 − 31
51 + 21	35 + 52	28 + 43	18 + 31	51 − 38	79 − 24	95 − 30	61 − 29	30 + 24
55 − 27	60 − 17	27 + 39	29 + 49	62 − 28	36 + 56	59 − 31	42 − 26	87 − 45
36 + 16	38 + 25	88 − 53	33 + 18	34 + 49	45 − 32	62 − 23	97 − 38	19 + 74

Finish

Vocabulary Review

Word List
- centimeter (cm)
- foot (ft)
- height
- inch (in.)
- length
- mental math
- meter (m)
- yard (yd)

Understand Vocabulary

Choose a term from the Word List to complete each sentence.

1. The length of your finger can best be measured

   in centimeters or _____.

2. 100 _____ equals 1 meter.

3. _____ is how tall an object is from bottom to top.

Write T for *true* or F for *false*.

4. _____ 1 yard is 5 feet long.

5. _____ 12 inches is 1 foot long.

6. _____ A centimeter is longer than a meter.

7. _____ You can do mental math in your head.

Use Vocabulary in Writing

8. Tell how to find the total length of two pieces of string. One piece of string is 12 inches long. The other piece is 9 inches long. Use terms from the Word List.

© Pearson Education, Inc. 2

Name _____

Set A _____

What is the distance around the front of the bookcase?

4 ft

3 ft

Add the lengths. Write an equation.

$4 + 3 + 4 + 3 =$ __14__

Distance around: __14__ feet

Reteaching

Write an equation to help solve.

1. What is the distance around the front of the crayon box?

12 cm

9 cm

Opposite sides have equal measures.

Distance around: _____ cm

Set B _____

A kite string is 27 feet long.
Some of the string is cut off.
Now the kite string is 18 feet long.
How many feet of kite string were cut off?
Write an equation and draw a picture.

$27 - ? = 18$ or $18 + ? = 27$

– 9 ft

15 16 17 18 19 20 21 22 23 24 25 26 27 28 29 30

__27__ – __9__ = __18__   __9__ feet

Write an equation using a ? for the unknown number. Then draw a picture to solve.

2. A piece of yarn is 42 inches long. Mia cuts some of it off. It is now 26 inches long. How much yarn did Mia cut off?

_____

A book measures 10 inches long. Another book measures 13 inches long. What is the total length of both books?

You can show 10 + 13 on a number line.

0   5   10   15   20   25   30

23 inches

Solve the problem using the number line.

3. One room in Jackie's house is 15 feet long. Another room is 9 feet long. What is the total length of both rooms?

0   5   10   15   20   25   30

Thinking Habits

Use Tools

Which of these tools can I use?

counters   paper and pencil
cubes   place-value blocks
measuring tools   string
number line   technology

Am I using the tool correctly?

Choose a tool to solve the problem.

4. Damon's shoelace is 45 inches long. His shoelace breaks. One piece is 28 inches long. How long is the other piece?

Explain your solution and why you chose the tool you used.

Name _____

1. A notebook has a length of 7 in. and a width of 5 in. What is the total distance around the notebook? Use the image below for help.

5 in.

7 in.　　　7 in.

5 in.

Distance around: _____ in.

2. Kate is 48 inches tall. Tom is 2 inches taller than Kate. James is 3 inches shorter than Tom.

How tall is James?

Ⓐ 45 inches　　　Ⓒ 50 inches

Ⓑ 47 inches　　　Ⓓ 53 inches

3. Alexis has a rope that is 7 feet long. Mariah's rope is 9 feet long. Sam's rope is 3 feet longer than Mariah's rope.

Use the measurements on the cards to complete each sentence.

| 2 feet | 5 feet | 12 feet |

Sam's rope is _____ long.

Alexis's rope is _____ shorter than Mariah's rope.

Sam's rope is _____ longer than Alexis's rope.

4. Joe rides his bike 18 miles. Then he rides 7 more miles.

Use the number line to find how far Joe rides. Then explain your work.

_____

_____

_____

_____

5. Pat says that each unknown equals 25 cm. Do you agree? Choose Yes or No.

47 cm + ? = 72 cm   ○ Yes   ○ No

? + 39 cm = 54 cm   ○ Yes   ○ No

99 cm − 64 cm = ?   ○ Yes   ○ No

93 cm − ? = 68 cm   ○ Yes   ○ No

6. Grace got a plant that was 34 cm tall. The plant grew and now it is 42 cm tall. How many centimeters did the plant grow?

Ⓐ   8 cm   Ⓒ   42 cm

Ⓑ   12 cm   Ⓓ   76 cm

7. Claire rides her bike 26 miles on Saturday and Sunday. She rides 8 miles on Sunday. How many miles does she ride on Saturday?

Write an equation to show the unknown.
Then use the number line to solve the problem.

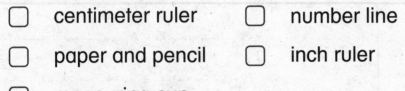

_____ ○ _____ = _____

_____ miles

8. Chris had a string that is 18 cm long. He cut off 7 cm. How much string is left?

A. Which of these tools could you use to solve the problem? Choose all that apply.

☐ centimeter ruler   ☐ number line

☐ paper and pencil   ☐ inch ruler

☐ measuring cup

B. Write an equation to show the unknown. Then draw a number line to solve.

_____ ○ _____ = _____

_____ cm

Name _____

Fishing Fun
Jim and his family go on a fishing trip.
They use a boat and fishing gear to help
them catch fish.

1. Jim takes this fishing box with him.
What is the distance around the front
of the fishing box? Write an equation
to help solve the problem. 2.MD.2.5, 2.OA.1.1

16 cm

31 cm

Distance around: _____ centimeters

2. Jim's fishing pole is 38 inches long.
His dad's fishing pole is 96 inches
long. How much shorter is Jim's
pole than his dad's pole? 2.MD.2.5, 2.OA.1.1

Part A Write a subtraction equation that shows
the problem.

_____

Part B Solve the problem.

_____ inches shorter

3. Jim catches a fish 49 yards away from the shore.
Later, he helps row the boat closer to the shore.
Now he is 27 yards away from the shore.
How many yards closer to shore is Jim now than
when he caught the fish? 2.MD.2.5, 2.OA.1.1

Part A Write an addition equation that shows the
problem.

_____

Part B Solve the problem.

_____ yards

4. Jim catches a silver fish that is 12 inches long. His sister catches a green fish that is 27 inches long.

What is the total length of both fish? Use the number line to solve. 🏛 2.MD.2.6

```
<—+++++++++++++++++++++++++++++++++++++++—>
   0   5  10  15  20  25  30  35  40
```

_____ inches

---

5. Jim has 27 yards of fishing line. He gives 12 yards of line to a friend. How many yards of line does Jim have left?

🏛 2.MD.2.6

```
<—+++++++++++++++++++++++++—>
   0   5  10  15  20  25  30
```

_____ yards

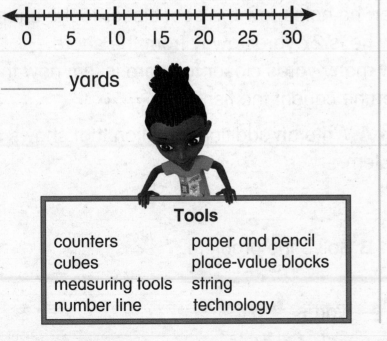

Tools

counters	paper and pencil
cubes	place-value blocks
measuring tools	string
number line	technology

---

6. Jim's family meets a man with a big boat. A parking spot at the dock is 32 feet long. Will the man's car and boat fit in the parking spot?

🏛 2.MD.2.5, 2.OA.1.1, MP.1.1

7 feet   2 feet   21 feet

Part A
What do you need to find? _____

_____

_____

Part B
What is the total length? Write an equation to solve.

_____ _____

Will the car and boat fit in the parking spot? Explain.

_____

_____

What tool did you use? _____

Graphs and Data

Essential Question: How can line plots, bar graphs, and picture graphs be used to show data and answer questions?

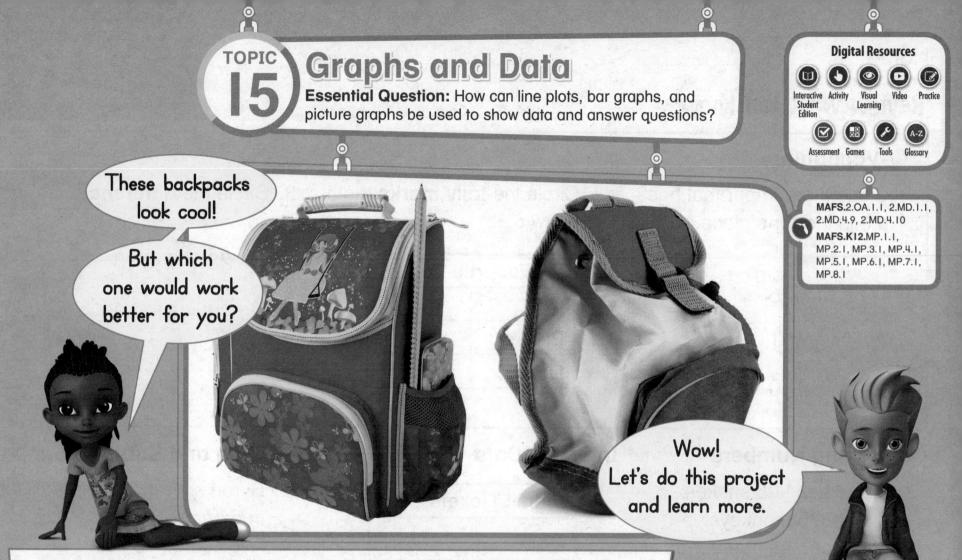

These backpacks look cool!

But which one would work better for you?

Wow! Let's do this project and learn more.

MAFS.2.OA.1.1, 2.MD.1.1, 2.MD.4.9, 2.MD.4.10
MAFS.K12.MP.1.1, MP.2.1, MP.3.1, MP.4.1, MP.5.1, MP.6.1, MP.7.1, MP.8.1

enVision STEM Project: Comparing Objects and Data

Find Out Work with a partner.
Compare two backpacks.
Which one holds more?
Which one has more parts?
Which one is easier to put on?
Think of other ways to compare.

Journal: Make a Book Show what you learn in a book. In your book, also:

• Tell one good thing and one bad thing about each backpack.

• Draw line plots, picture graphs, and bar graphs to show and compare data.

Name _____

Review What You Know

A-Z Vocabulary

1. Circle the number that has a 6 in the **tens** place.

406

651

160

2. Circle the **tally marks** that show 6.

Favorite Toy	
Car	$\cancel{||||}$ ||
Blocks	||||
Doll	$\cancel{||||}$	

3. Circle the **difference**.

$$22 - 9 = 13$$

$$34 + 61 = 95$$

Comparing Numbers

4. A zoo has 405 snakes. It has 375 monkeys. Compare the number of snakes to the number of monkeys.

Write > or <.

405 $\bigcirc$ 375

Interpret Data

5.

Picnic Tickets Sold	
Jean	16
Paulo	18
Fatima	12

Who sold the most picnic tickets?

_____

Addition and Subtraction

6. Byron scores 24 points in a game. Ava scores 16 points in the same game. How many more points does Byron score than Ava?

_____ more points

Name _____

PROJECT 15A

What types of flowers grow in your neighborhood?

Project: Graph Data About Flowers

PROJECT 15B

How many birds do you see every day?

Project: Create a Bird-Watching Poster

PROJECT 15C

Why should you plan a Florida vacation?

Project: Make a Florida Travel Brochure

Before watching the video, think:

How do you know what size clothing you should wear? Is there a way you can find out without trying the clothes on?

MAFS.K12.MP.4.1 Model with mathematics. **Also MP.5.1, MP.6.1**
MAFS.2.MD.4.10 Draw a picture graph and a bar graph (with single-unit scale) to represent a data set with up to four categories. Solve simple put-together, take-apart, and compare problems using information presented in a bar graph.
Also 2.MD.4.9

© Pearson Education, Inc. 2

Solve & Share

Find four objects that are each shorter than 9 inches. Measure the length of each object to the nearest inch. Record the measurements in the table.

Then plot the data on the number line.

Which object is longest? Which is shortest?

I can ...

measure the lengths of objects, then make a line plot to organize the data.

MAFS.2.MD.4.9 Generate measurement data by measuring lengths of several objects to the nearest whole unit, or by making repeated measurements of the same object. Show the measurements by making a line plot, where the horizontal scale is marked off in whole-number units. **Also 2.MD.1.1**
MAFS.K12.MP.2.1, MP.5.1, MP.6.1

Object	Length in Inches

Lengths of Objects

Number of Inches

2 inches long

You can measure the length of objects. This glue stick is 2 inches long.

You can use a table to record the measurement **data**.

Object	Length in Inches
Glue Stick	2
String	4
Feather	6
Scissors	4

You can make a **line plot** to show the data. Place a dot over the number that shows each length.

The two dots above the 4 tell me that two objects are 4 inches long.

Lengths of Objects

0 1 2 3 4 5 6 7 8

Number of Inches

Convince Me! Measure the length of your pencil to the nearest inch. Record your measurement on the line plot above. How does it change the data?

☆ **Guided Practice** ☆ Use a ruler to measure each object in inches. Record each length in the table. Then make a line plot. Show each length on the line plot.

1. ___4___ inches long

___ inches long

2.

Object	Length (in.)
Marker	4
Crayon	

Lengths of Objects

0 1 2 3 4 5

Number of Inches

© Pearson Education, Inc. 2

Topic 15 | Lesson 1

Independent Practice

Use a ruler to measure each object in inches. Record each length in the table. Show each length on the line plot.

3. The paintbrush is _____ inches long.

4. The chalk is _____ inches long.

5. The straw is _____ inches long.

6. The feather is _____ inches long.

7.

Object	Length in Inches
Paintbrush	
Chalk	
Straw	
Feather	

Lengths of Objects

0   1   2   3   4   5   6   7   8
Number of Inches

8. **Be Precise** Sophia measured the lengths of her colored pencils and made a table. Use the data to make a line plot.

You can use dots or Xs to record data in a line plot.

Pencil Color	Length in Inches
Red	4
Blue	3
Green	7
Yellow	9

Lengths of Pencils

← | + | + | + | + | + | + | + | + | + →
0   1   2   3   4   5   6   7   8   9

Number of Inches

9. What is the length of the shortest pencil? Explain.

_____

_____

10. **Higher Order Thinking** What are the lengths of the two pencils have a total length of 16 inches? Explain.

_____

_____

_____

11. ⚑ **Assessment Practice** Measure the length of the purple pencil in inches. Write the length below. Record your measurement on the line plot above in Item 8. 🏆 2.MD.4.9

____ inches

© Pearson Education, Inc. 2

Name _____

Solve & Share

Measure the length of your shoe to the nearest inch. Then use your data and data from your class to make a line plot.

Tell one thing you learn from the data.

I can ...
measure the lengths of objects, then make a line plot to organize the data.

MAFS.2.MD.4.9 Generate measurement data by measuring lengths of several objects to the nearest whole unit, or by making repeated measurements of the same object. Show the measurements by making a line plot, where the horizontal scale is marked off in whole-number units. **Also 2.MD.1.1**
MAFS.K12.MP.2.1, MP.4.1, MP.6.1

Shoe Lengths

```
 2   3   4   5   6   7   8   9   10
```
Number of Inches

Some students measure their heights. They record the data in a table. Are there any patterns in the data?

Student Heights in Inches

46	48	47	49
49	47	46	48
48	49	50	47
49	48	49	51

You can make a line plot to look for patterns.

To make a line plot, draw a number line, and write a title and labels to fit your data.

Students' Heights

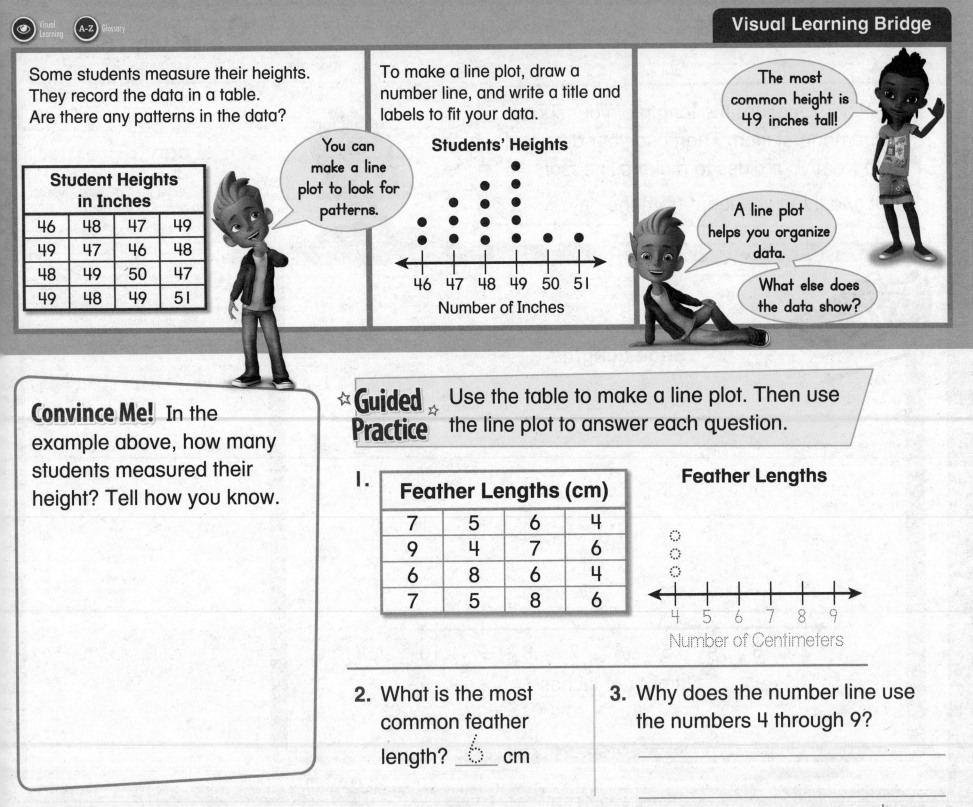

Number of Inches

The most common height is 49 inches tall!

A line plot helps you organize data.

What else does the data show?

Convince Me! In the example above, how many students measured their height? Tell how you know.

☆ **Guided Practice** ☆ Use the table to make a line plot. Then use the line plot to answer each question.

1.

Feather Lengths (cm)

7	5	6	4
9	4	7	6
6	8	6	4
7	5	8	6

Feather Lengths

4 5 6 7 8 9

Number of Centimeters

2. What is the most common feather length? __6__ cm

3. Why does the number line use the numbers 4 through 9?

© Pearson Education, Inc. 2

Independent Practice

Collect data and use the data to complete the line plot. Then use the line plot to solve the problems.

4. Measure the length of your pencil in centimeters. Collect pencil-length data from your classmates. Make a line plot with the data.

Title: _____

Make a line plot using the data you collect.

Label: _____

5. What is the length of the longest pencil?

_____

6. What is the sum of the lengths of the shortest and longest pencils?

_____

7. What is the difference in lengths between the shortest and longest pencils?

_____

8. What is the most common pencil length?

_____

9. **A-Z Vocabulary** Use these words to complete the sentences.   **longest   line plot   order**

A _____ can help you see the data in _____ .

A line plot can show the lengths of the shortest and _____ objects.

Model Use the data in the table to complete the line plot. Then use the line plot to solve the problems.

10.

Crayon Lengths in Centimeters			
6	7	5	6
7	5	7	6
7	8	6	5
5	6	7	6
8	8	6	8

Title: _____

Label: _____

What numbers will you use to make your line plot?

11. **Higher Order Thinking** Measure the length of one of your crayons in centimeters, 5 different times. Make a line plot of the data on a separate sheet of paper. Did you get the same measurement each time? Explain.

_____
_____
_____

12. 🔵 **Assessment Practice** Measure the length of the blue crayon to the nearest centimeter. Write the length below. 2.MD.4.9

_____

Then record your measurement on the line plot above that you made in Item 10.

© Pearson Education, Inc. 2

Solve & Share

The graph shows the number of birthdays in each season for a class.

Use the graph to write the number of birthdays in the table. How many more birthdays are celebrated during spring, fall, and winter than during summer? Be ready to explain how you know.

Lesson 15-3
Bar Graphs

I can ...
draw bar graphs and use them to solve problems.

MAFS.2.MD.4.10 Draw a picture graph and a bar graph (with single-unit scale) to represent a data set with up to four categories. Solve simple put-together, take-apart, and compare problems using information presented in a bar graph. **Also 2.OA.1.1**
MAFS.K12.MP.2.1, MP.3.1, MP.4.1

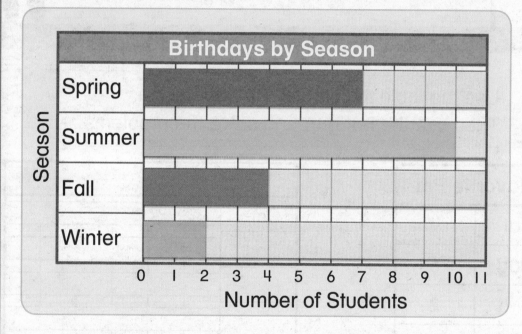

Birthdays by Season

Spring	
Summer	
Fall	
Winter	

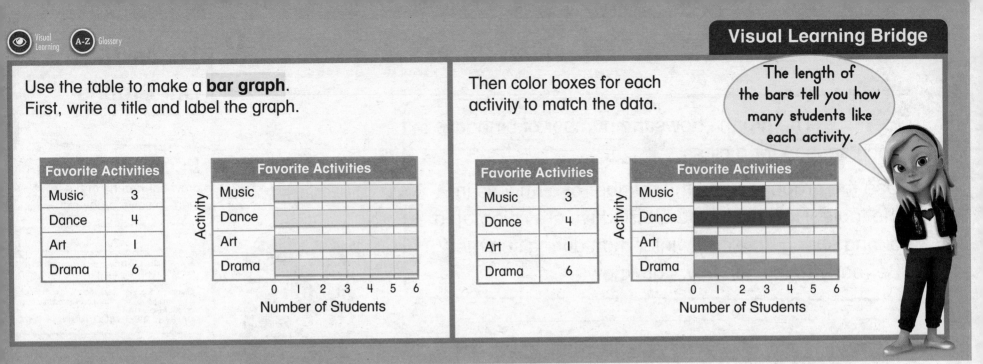

Use the table to make a **bar graph**.
First, write a title and label the graph.

Then color boxes for each activity to match the data.

The length of the bars tell you how many students like each activity.

Convince Me! Which activity did the most students choose? Explain how you know.

☆ **Guided Practice** ☆ Use the table to complete the bar graph. Then use the bar graph to solve the problems.

Favorite Pet	
Cat	4
Dog	6
Bird	2
Turtle	3

1. How many students chose cat?

   4

2. How many students chose bird or dog?

© Pearson Education, Inc. 2

Name _____

Independent Practice ☆ Use the bar graph to solve the problems.

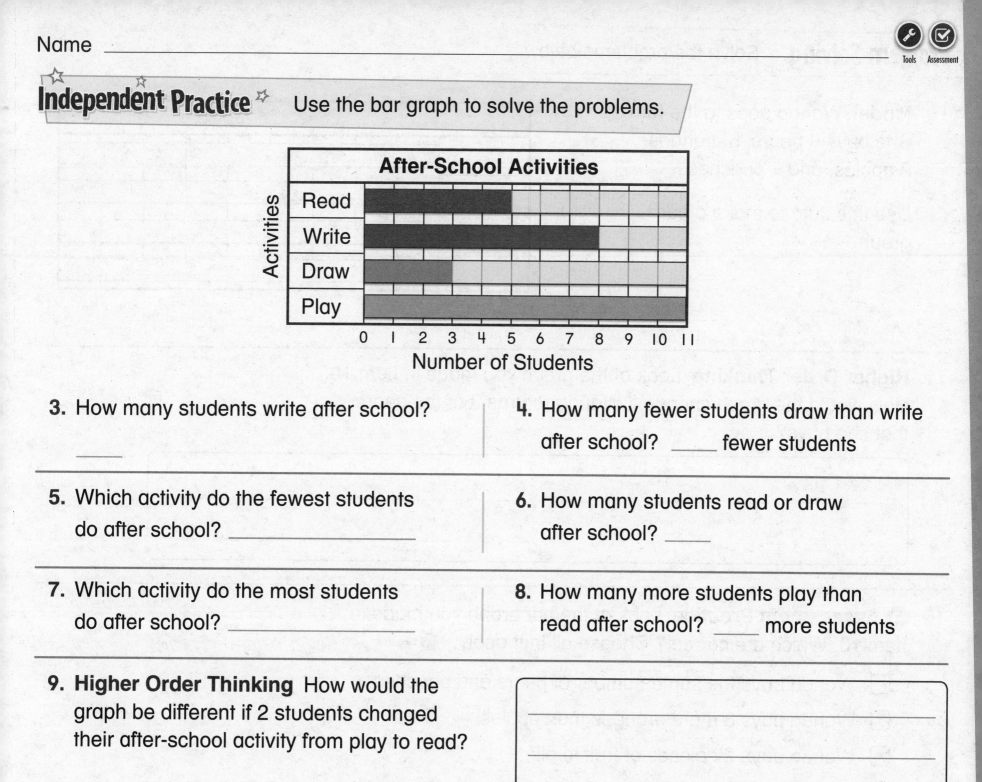

After-School Activities

Activities: Read, Write, Draw, Play

Number of Students (0 to 11)

3. How many students write after school?

   _____

4. How many fewer students draw than write after school? _____ fewer students

5. Which activity do the fewest students do after school? _____

6. How many students read or draw after school? _____

7. Which activity do the most students do after school? _____

8. How many more students play than read after school? _____ more students

9. **Higher Order Thinking** How would the graph be different if 2 students changed their after-school activity from play to read?

   _____
   _____
   _____

☆ Solve the problems below.

10. **Model** Wanda goes to the farm.
    She buys 8 pears, 5 oranges,
    2 apples, and 9 peaches.

    Use this data to make a bar
    graph.

11. **Higher Order Thinking** Look at the graph you made in Item 10.
    How would the graph change if Wanda returns 3 of the pears
    that she buys?

12. 🕐 **Assessment Practice** Look at the bar graph you made in
    Item 10. Which are correct? Choose all that apply. 🕐 2.MD.4.10

    ☐ Wanda buys the same number of pears and peaches.

    ☐ Wanda buys 3 more oranges than apples.

    ☐ Wanda buys 24 pieces of fruit in all.

    ☐ Wanda buys 3 fewer oranges than pears.

Name _____

Solve & Share

The picture graph shows the favorite subjects of a class. Draw a smiley face on the graph to show your favorite subject. Then interview two classmates and add their data.

How many students responded to the survey?
Which subject do most students like best?
How many students like math or science best?

I can ...
draw picture graphs and use them to solve problems.

MAFS.2.MD.4.10 Draw a picture graph and a bar graph (with single-unit scale) to represent a data set with up to four categories. Solve simple put-together, take-apart, and compare problems using information presented in a bar graph. Also 2.OA.1.1
MAFS.K12.MP.3.1, MP.4.1, MP.8.1

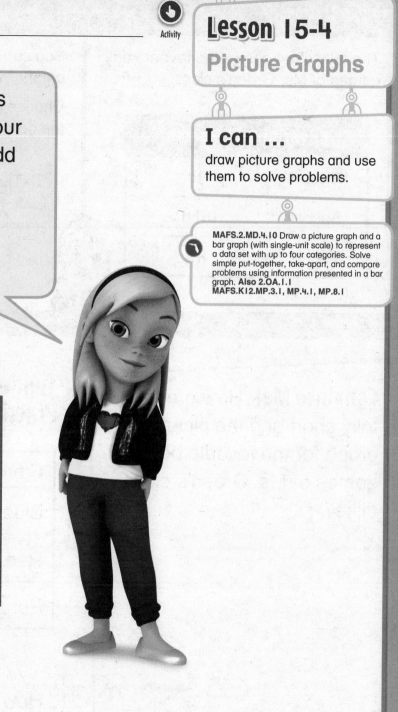

Favorite School Subject

	1	2	3	4	5	6	7	8
Reading	☺	☺	☺	☺				
Math	☺	☺	☺	☺	☺			
Science	☺	☺	☺					
Social Studies	☺							

Number of Students

The tally chart shows the favorite ball games of Ms. Green's class.

Favorite Ball Games	
Baseball	II
Soccer	ᚾᚼᚾᚼ III
Tennis	IIII

You can show the same data in another way.

Choose a **symbol** to represent the data.

The symbol will be ☖. Each ☖ represents 1 student.

A **picture graph** uses pictures to show data.

You can draw the symbols to show the data.

8 students chose soccer!

Favorite Ball Games	
Baseball	☖ ☖
Soccer	☖ ☖ ☖ ☖ ☖ ☖ ☖ ☖
Tennis	☖ ☖ ☖ ☖

Each ☖ = 1 student

Convince Me! How are the tally chart and the picture graph for the favorite ball games of Ms. Green's class alike?

☆ **Guided Practice** ☆ Use the tally chart to complete the picture graph. Then use the picture graph to solve the problems.

Favorite Colors	
Blue	ᚾᚼᚾ
Red	ᚾᚼᚾ I
Purple	III

Favorite Colors	
Blue	╲ ╲ ╲ ╲ ╲
Red	
Purple	

Each ✏ = 1 vote

1. How many students like blue or red best?

___||___

2. Which color is the favorite of most students?

_____

© Pearson Education, Inc. 2

Topic 15 | Lesson 4

Name _____

Independent Practice

Use the tally chart to complete the picture graph.
Then use the picture graph to solve the problems.

3.

Favorite Season	
Spring	IIII
Summer	THL THL
Fall	THL I
Winter	II

Favorite Season	
Spring	
Summer	
Fall	
Winter	

Each 👤 = I vote

4. How many students like fall best?

_____

5. Which season do exactly 4 students like best? _____

6. Which season do the fewest students like?

_____

7. How many fewer students voted for winter than for summer? _____

8. How many more students voted for summer than for spring and winter combined? _____ more students

9. How many students like the season with the most votes? _____

10. **Higher Order Thinking** Look at the picture graph above. How would the graph change if 2 students changed their votes from summer to fall?

_____

_____

Use the tally chart to complete the picture graph.
Use the picture graph to solve the problems.

11. **Model** Bob made a tally chart to show the trees in a park.

Trees in the Park	
Birch	III
Oak	卌 I
Maple	卌
Pine	II

Trees in the Park	
Birch	
Oak	
Maple	
Pine	

Each 🌲 = 1 tree

You can model data using a picture graph.

12. **enVision® STEM** Birch, oak, maple, and pine trees are common in North America. Which type of tree is most common in the park?

_____

13. **Higher Order Thinking** How many birch and maple trees are there in all?

_____

14. 🌴 **Assessment Practice** Draw a picture graph to show the data in the table. 2.MD.4.10

Favorite Drink	
Milk	III
Juice	IIII
Water	I

Each 🥤 = 1 vote

Name _____

Solve & Share

7 students voted for Turtle as their favorite pond animal.
10 students voted for Frog. 4 students voted for Fish.
Make a picture graph to show the data.
Write two things you notice about the data.

I can ...
draw conclusions from graphs.

MAFS.2.MD.4.10 Draw a picture graph and a bar graph (with single-unit scale) to represent a data set with up to four categories. Solve simple put-together, take-apart, and compare problems using information presented in a bar graph. **Also 2.OA.1.1**
MAFS.K12.MP.1.1, MP.3.1, MP.7.1

Favorite Pond Animals

Turtle	
Frog	
Fish	

Each ★ = 1 vote

1. _____

2. _____

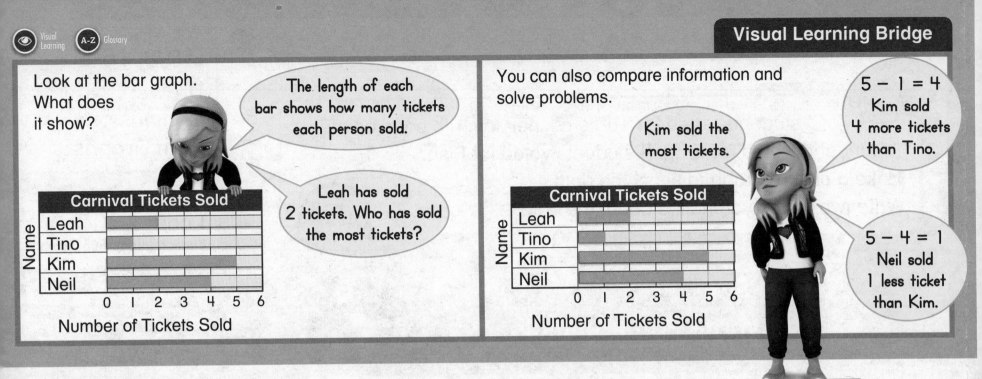

Look at the bar graph. What does it show?

The length of each bar shows how many tickets each person sold.

Leah has sold 2 tickets. Who has sold the most tickets?

Carnival Tickets Sold

You can also compare information and solve problems.

Kim sold the most tickets.

$5 - 1 = 4$
Kim sold 4 more tickets than Tino.

$5 - 4 = 1$
Neil sold 1 less ticket than Kim.

Carnival Tickets Sold

Convince Me! Look at the graph above. How many tickets did Kim and Neil sell in all? How do you know?

☆ **Guided Practice** ☆ Use the bar graph to solve the problems.

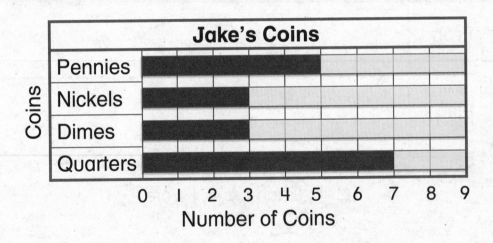

Jake's Coins

1. How many pennies does Jake have?

5

2. Jake spends 3 of his quarters. How many does he have left?

_____

© Pearson Education, Inc. 2

Topic 15 | Lesson 5

Name _____

Independent Practice   Use the bar graph to solve the problems.

3. How many absences were there in all on Tuesday and Thursday?

_____

Absences at School

4. Were fewer students absent on Monday or Friday? How many fewer?

_____

5. Three of the students absent on Friday were boys. How many girls were absent on Friday?

_____

6. On which two days were the same number of students absent?

_____

7. Were more students absent on Wednesday or Thursday? How many more?

_____

8. **Higher Order Thinking** The graph shows the number of absences last week. This week, there are 19 absences. Compare the number of absences this week to the number of absences last week.

_____

9. Make Sense Complete each sentence.

The farm has _____ cows and _____ horses.

The farm has _____ goats and _____ sheep.

10. The sheep and goats are kept in the same pen. How many farm animals are in that pen?

_____

11. Suppose 3 new baby goats are born. Then how many goats will the farmer have?

_____

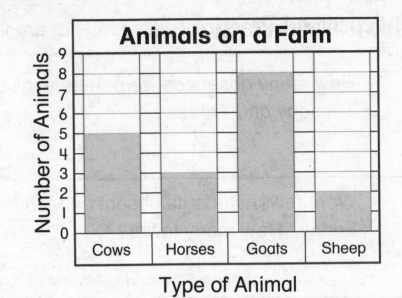

Animals on a Farm

Number of Animals (vertical axis, 0–9)

Cows, Horses, Goats, Sheep

Type of Animal

12. How many fewer horses than cows are on the farm?

_____ fewer horses

13. Write the order of animals on the farm from the greatest number to the least number.

_____

14. Higher Order Thinking Do you think the bars on a bar graph should all be the same color? Explain.

_____

15. 🔵 **Assessment Practice** The farmer wants to buy some sheep. He wants to have as many sheep as cows. How many more sheep should the farmer buy? 🐢 2.MD.4.10

_____ more sheep

© Pearson Education, Inc. 2

Solve & Share

Make a picture graph to show how many connecting cubes, counters, and ones cubes you have. Then write and solve a problem about your data.

Math Tools

Connecting Cubes	
Counters	
Ones Cubes	

I can ...
reason about data in bar graphs and picture graphs to write and solve problems.

MAFS.K12.MP.2.1 Reason abstractly and quantitatively. **Also MP.1.1, MP.3.1, MP.6.1, MP.8.1**
MAFS.2.MD.4.10 Draw a picture graph and a bar graph (with single-unit scale) to represent a data set with up to four categories. Solve simple put-together, take-apart, and compare problems using information presented in a bar graph. **Also 2.OA.1.1**

Each _____ = I math tool

Thinking Habits

What do the symbols mean?

How are the numbers in the problem related?

_____

_____

_____

The bar graph shows the number of stamps each student has collected.

Write and solve a problem about the data in the bar graph.

Stamp Collections

Student	
Ben	
Lara	
David	
Gail	

0 1 2 3 4 5 6 7 8 9 10 11 12 13 14 15 16 17 18 19 20 21 22 23 24 25
Number of Stamps

How can I use reasoning to write and solve a problem?

I can look at the bars to see how many stamps each student has.

I can write a problem to compare the number of stamps two students have.

My Problem

How many more stamps does Lara have than Gail?

25 - 15 = 10
10 more stamps

Convince Me! Use reasoning to write your own problem about the data in the graph. Then solve it.

Guided Practice

Use the bar graph to write and solve problems.

Meytal's Closet

Item	
Shorts	
Shirts	
Pants	
Skirts	

0 1 2 3 4 5 6 7 8 9 10 11 12 13 14 15 16
Number of Items

1. How many shirts and skirts are there in all?

___ ◯ ___ = ___

2. ___

___ ◯ ___ = ___

Name _____

Tools   Assessment

Independent Practice ☆ Use the bar graph to write and solve problems.

3. _____

_____

_____

____ ◯ ____ = ____

_____

_____

4. _____

_____

____ ◯ ____ = ____

_____

_____

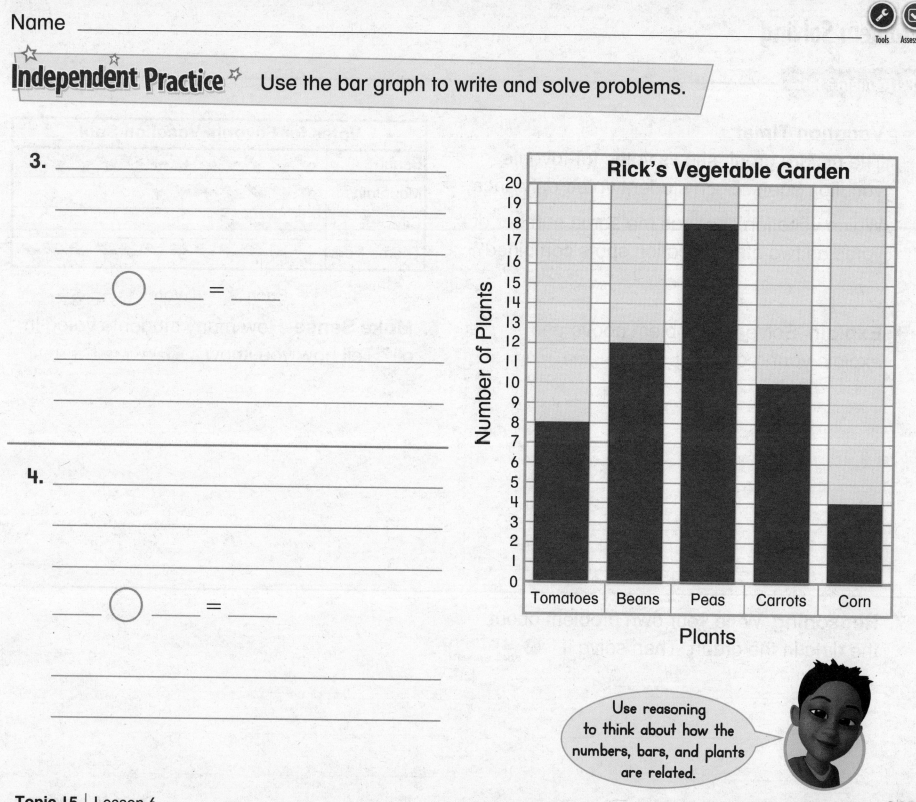

Rick's Vegetable Garden

Number of Plants

20
19
18
17
16
15
14
13
12
11
10
9
8
7
6
5
4
3
2
1
0

Tomatoes | Beans | Peas | Carrots | Corn

Plants

Use reasoning to think about how the numbers, bars, and plants are related.

Topic 15 | Lesson 6

six hundred sixty-three   **663**

Problem Solving

Vacation Time!

The picture graph shows votes for favorite vacation spots. Each student voted only once.

Which vacation spot has the same number of votes as two other vacation spots combined?

Votes for Favorite Vacation Spot	
Beach	✓✓✓✓✓✓✓✓✓✓
Mountains	✓✓✓✓✓
City	✓✓✓
Theme Park	✓✓✓✓✓✓✓✓✓✓✓

Each ✓ = 1 vote

5. Explain Solve the problem above and explain your reasoning. ● 2.MD.4.10, 2.OA.1.1, MP.3.1

_____

_____

_____

_____

6. Make Sense How many students voted in all? Tell how you know. ● 2.MD.4.10, 2.OA.1.1, MP.1.1

_____

_____

_____

_____

7. Reasoning Write your own problem about the data in the graph. Then solve it. ● 2.MD.4.10, 2.OA.1.1, MP.2.1

____ ◯ ____ = ____

_____

_____

© Pearson Education, Inc. 2

Name _____

Find a Match

Find a partner. Point to a clue. Read the clue.

Look below the clues to find a match. Write the clue letter in the box next to the match.

Find a match for every clue.

I can ...
add and subtract within 100.

MAFS.2.NBT.2.5

Clues

A The difference is less than 16.

B The sum equals $43 + 25$.

C The difference equals $75 - 46$.

D The sum equals $53 + 20$.

E The difference equals $96 - 19$.

F The sum equals 75.

G The sum is between 60 and 65.

H The difference is between 25 and 28.

□ $39 + 24$	□ $81 - 52$	□ $33 + 42$	□ $35 + 38$
□ $73 - 59$	□ $67 - 40$	□ $88 - 11$	□ $17 + 51$

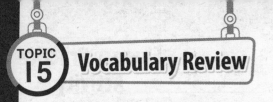

Vocabulary Review

A-Z
Glossary

Word List
- bar graph
- data
- line plot
- picture graph
- symbol

Understand Vocabulary

Label each data display. Write *line plot*, *bar graph*, or *picture graph.*

1.

Favorite Activities

Activity

| Music | Dance | Art | Drama |

Number of Students
0 1 2 3 4 5 6

_____

2.

Favorite Ball Games	
Baseball	🚹🚹
Soccer	🚹🚹🚹🚹🚹🚹🚹🚹
Tennis	🚹🚹🚹🚹

Each 🚹 = 1 student

_____

3.

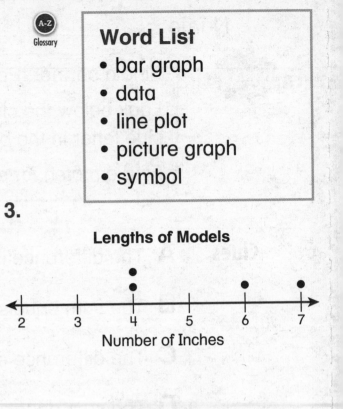

Lengths of Models

Number of Inches

_____

Use Vocabulary in Writing

4. Look at the graph in Item 2. Use words to tell how to find which ball game is the most popular. Use terms from the Word List.

© Pearson Education, Inc. 2

Name _____

Set A

Line plots show and organize data.
Use an inch ruler. Measure the length of
the toy car. Then record the measurement
in the table.

Toy	Length in Inches
Car	3
Airplane	5
Doll	5
Block	1

Place a dot over the number that shows
the length of each toy.

Length of Toys

Number of Inches

Reteaching

Complete the table and show
the data on a line plot.

1. Use an inch ruler. Measure the length of
the pencil. Then record the measurement
in the table.

Object	Length in Inches
Pencil	
Stapler	6
Scissors	6
Eraser	3

2. Make a line plot to show each length in
the table.

Length of Objects

Number of Inches

TOPIC 15

You can make a bar graph to show the data in a table.

Students voted for their favorite nut. The table shows the number of votes.

Favorite Nut	
Peanut	7
Almond	4
Cashew	5

Color one space for each vote in the bar graph.

Then use the graph to solve the problem.

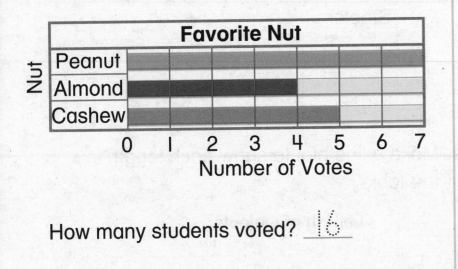

How many students voted? __16__

Use the table to complete the bar graph. Then solve each problem.

3.

Favorite Yogurt	
Lemon	3
Vanilla	7
Banana	6

4. How many more students voted for vanilla than banana? _____

5. How many fewer students voted for lemon than vanilla? _____

Name _____

Set C

A picture graph uses pictures or symbols to show data.

The tally chart shows votes for favorite sea animals.

Favorite Sea Animals	
Whale	⊦⊦⊦⊦ I
Dolphin	II
Seal	IIII

Use the data to make a picture graph.
Each ⚲ stands for 1 vote.

Favorite Sea Animals	
Whale	⚲⚲⚲⚲⚲⚲
Dolphin	⚲⚲
Seal	⚲⚲⚲⚲

Each ⚲ = 1 vote

Which sea animal has the fewest votes?

dolphin

Use the tally chart to complete the picture graph.
Then solve each problem.

6.

Favorite Birds	
Blue Jay	⊦⊦⊦⊦
Robin	⊦⊦⊦⊦ III
Seagull	⊦⊦⊦⊦ ⊦⊦⊦⊦

Favorite Birds	
Blue Jay	
Robin	
Seagull	

Each 🐦 = 1 vote

7. How many votes did seagull get?

_____

8. Which bird had the fewest votes?

_____

Thinking Habits

Reasoning

What do the symbols mean?

How are the numbers in the problem related?

How can I write a word problem using the information that is given?

How do the numbers in my problem relate to each other?

How can I use a word problem to show what an equation means?

Use the picture graph to solve each problem. Each student voted once.

Favorite Winter Sport	
Skiing	✻ ✻ ✻ ✻ ✻ ✻ ✻
Snowboarding	✻ ✻ ✻ ✻ ✻ ✻ ✻ ✻ ✻ ✻
Skating	✻ ✻ ✻ ✻ ✻ ✻ ✻ ✻
Ice Fishing	✻ ✻ ✻ ✻

Each ✻ = I vote

9. How many fewer students chose ice fishing than snowboarding? _____

10. Write and solve your own problem about the data.

_____

_____

____ ◯ ____ = ____

© Pearson Education, Inc. 2

Name _____

1. Pam has 5 pennies, 2 nickels, 8 dimes, and 9 quarters. Show this data in the bar graph below. Draw the bars.

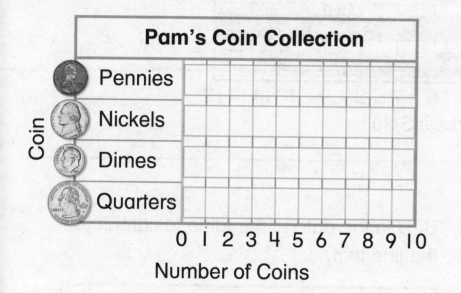

Pam's Coin Collection

Coin: Pennies, Nickels, Dimes, Quarters

0 1 2 3 4 5 6 7 8 9 10

Number of Coins

2. Use the bar graph you made above. Pam spends 5 of her dimes to buy an apple. Now how many dimes does Pam have left?

Ⓐ   13

Ⓑ   5

Ⓒ   3

Ⓓ   0

3. Is each sentence about the picture graph correct? Choose Yes or No.

Favorite Camp Activity	
Crafts	🧍 🧍 🧍
Swimming	🧍 🧍 🧍 🧍 🧍
Archery	🧍 🧍
Tennis	🧍 🧍 🧍 🧍 🧍 🧍

Each 🧍 = 1 camper

7 students voted for tennis.   ○ Yes ○ No

16 students voted in all.   ○ Yes ○ No

2 more students voted for swimming than for crafts.   ○ Yes ○ No

3 fewer students voted for tennis than for crafts.   ○ Yes ○ No

4. How many more tickets did Kendra sell than Leon?

Ⓐ 5

Ⓑ 6

Ⓒ 11

Ⓓ 17

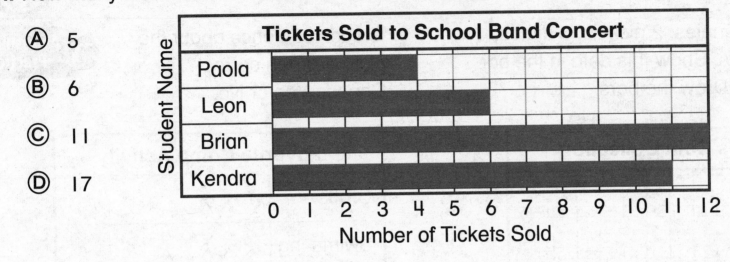

Tickets Sold to School Band Concert

Student Name / Number of Tickets Sold

Paola, Leon, Brian, Kendra

0 1 2 3 4 5 6 7 8 9 10 11 12

---

5. Complete the table and the line plot.

A. Use a centimeter ruler. Measure the length of the crayon to the nearest centimeter. Write the length in the table below.

Crayon Lengths in Centimeters			
5	7	7	8
4	7	5	

B. Use the data in the table to complete the line plot.

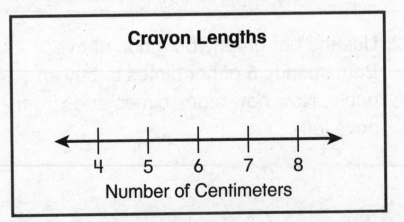

Crayon Lengths

4 5 6 7 8

Number of Centimeters

What is the difference in length between the shortest and longest crayon?

© Pearson Education, Inc. 2

Topic 15 | Assessment Practice

6. Scott is making a picture graph from the data in the tally chart.
How many symbols should he draw in the bottom row?

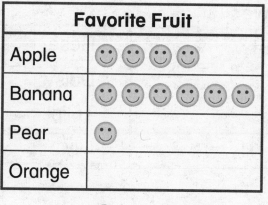

Favorite Fruit	
Apple	IIII
Banana	ꟼꟼꟼꟼ I
Pear	I
Orange	ꟼꟼꟼꟼ

Favorite Fruit	
Apple	☺ ☺ ☺ ☺
Banana	☺ ☺ ☺ ☺ ☺ ☺
Pear	☺
Orange	

Each ☺ = I student

Ⓐ 3   Ⓑ 4   Ⓒ 5   Ⓓ 6

7. Mary gets new stamps every month.
The bar graph shows the number of stamps she collects each month.

Which statements are true? Choose all that apply.

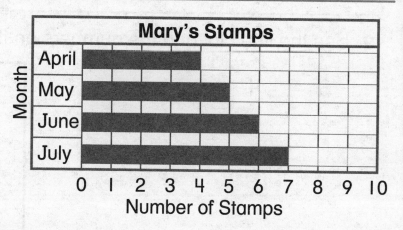

☐ Mary collects I more stamp in May than she does in April.

☐ Mary collects 2 fewer stamps in June than she does in July.

☐ Mary collects a total of I I stamps in May and June.

☐ Mary collects one additional stamp each month from May to July.

☐ Mary collects the most stamps in June.

8. Use the tally chart to complete the picture graph.
Then use the picture graph to solve the problems.

Favorite Flower	
Rose	卌 I
Daisy	III
Tulip	卌
Lily	卌 III

Favorite Flower	
Rose	
Daisy	
Tulip	
Lily	

Each 🌸 = I vote

How many students voted for Lily? _____

Which flower is the least favorite? _____

9. Use the line plot and the numbers on the cards to complete each sentence.

3 pencils are _____ inches long.

The longest pencil is _____ inches long.

The shortest pencil is _____ inches long.

The difference between the shortest and longest pencil is _____ inches.

© Pearson Education, Inc. 2 **Topic 15** | Assessment Practice

Name _____

School Surveys

Some students asked their classmates different questions.

George asked his classmates to vote for their favorite lunch. This table shows the results.

Favorite Lunch

Favorite Lunch	
Taco	5
Pizza	8
Hamburger	9
Salad	6

1. Use the table to complete the bar graph. 🐢 2.MD.4.10, MP.4.1, MP.6.1

2. Use the Favorite Lunch table to complete the picture graph. 🐢 2.MD.4.10, MP.4.1, MP.6.1

Favorite Lunch	
Taco	
Pizza	
Hamburger	
Salad	

Each ✔ = 1 student

3. Use the graphs you made to answer these questions. 🐢 2.MD.4.10, 2.OA.1.1, MP.1.1, MP.2.1

How many students chose salad as their favorite lunch? _____

How many fewer students chose taco than hamburger? _____ fewer students

How would the bar graph change if two more students chose taco?

_____

_____

4. Write and solve a math story about the Favorite Lunch graphs you made.

2.MD.4.10, 2.OA.1.1, MP.1.1, MP.6.1

Part A

Use the bar graph or the picture graph about favorite lunches to write a math story problem. The problem should include addition or subtraction.

_____

_____

_____

Part B

Solve your math story problem. Explain how you solved the problem.

_____

_____

_____

_____

5. Gina asked her classmates to measure the length of their favorite storybook in inches. She recorded their measurements in this table.

2.MD.4.9, 2.OA.1.1, MP.4.1, MP.6.1, MP.7.1

Lengths of Books in Inches			
12	9	8	10
6	10	11	9
10	9	9	12
12	10	7	7

Part A

Use the table to make a line plot.

Part B

What is the difference in length between the longest and shortest books?

_____ inches

© Pearson Education, Inc. 2

Photographs

Every effort has been made to secure permission and provide appropriate credit for photographic material. The publisher deeply regrets any omission and pledges to correct errors called to its attention in subsequent editions.

Unless otherwise acknowledged, all photographs are the property of Pearson Education, Inc.

Photo locators denoted as follows: Top (T), Center (C), Bottom (B), Left (L), Right (R), Background (Bkgd)

1 (TL) Africa Studio/Fotolia, (TC) Africa Studio/Fotolia, (TR) karandaev/Fotolia, (BL) Lori Martin/Shutterstock; (BR) An Nguyen/Shutterstock, **3** (T) 123RF, (C) Sean Pavone/Shutterstock, (B) Trinet Uzun/Shutterstock; **4** Sergey Sarychev/Shutterstock, Lesinka372/Shutterstock, Corinna Huter/Shutterstock, 123RF; **57** (TL) Shadowmac/Shutterstock, (TR) Rose Thompson/Shutterstock, (BL) Tory Kallman/Shutterstock, (BR) Jo Crebbin/Shutterstock; **59** (T) Steve Byland/Shutterstock, (B) Islavicek/Shutterstock; **60** (T) Smileus/Shutterstock, (B) 123RF; **89** (L) FiCo74/Fotolia; (R) Antonio Scarpi/Fotolia, **91** (T) Pisaphotography/Shutterstock, (C) Aviation Images/Alamy Stock Photo, (B) Lazyllama/Shutterstock; **92** (T) S_Rouse/Shutterstock, (C) Diane C Macdonald/Shutterstock, (B) Russo Photography/Shutterstock; **133** Beboy/Shutterstock; **135** (T) Echo/Juice Images/Getty Images, (B) Peter Leahy/Shutterstock; **136** (T) Universal Images Group North America LLC/Alamy Stock Photo, (B) Charles O. Cecil/Alamy Stock Photo; **185** Deborah Benbrook/Fotolia; **187** (T) Cturtletrax/iStock/Getty Images, (C) Inxti/Shutterstock, (B) Horizon International Images Limited/Alamy Stock Photo; **188** (T) Evgeny Atamanenko/Shutterstock (C) Thomas M Perkins/Shutterstock, (B) Nisakorn Neera/Shutterstock; **233** GlebStock/Shutterstock; **235** (T) Joe McDonald/Corbis Documentary/Getty Images, (B) Hero Images Inc./Alamy Stock Photo; **236** (T) Ivaylo Sarayski/Alamy Stock Photo, (B) Vchal/Shutterstock; **277** Paylessimages/Fotolia; **279** (T) Kiselev Andrey Valerevich/Shutterstock, (C) Mr. Ned Klezmer/Shutterstock, (B) IrinaK/Shutterstock; **280** Mikhail Zahranichny/Shutterstock; Good Shop Background/Shutterstock; **325** Ambient Ideas/Shutterstock; **327** (T) Chuck Pefley/Alamy Stock Photo, (B) Masterchief_Productions; **328** (B) (T) Will Hart/PhotoEdit, Christopher Villano/Image Source/Alamy Stock Photo; **373** Es0lex/Fotolia; **375** (T) Christos Georghiou/Shutterstock,(C) Gilles Barbier/imageBROKER/Alamy Stock Photo, (B) Brian J. Skerry/National Geographic/Getty Images; **376** People Image Studio/Shutterstock; Brandon Alms/Shutterstock, Fashion iconography/Shutterstock; **429** Tonyz20/Shutterstock; **431** (T) Karin Hildebrand Lau/Alamy Stock Photo, (B) Richard Paul Kane/Shutterstock; **432** (T) Nagel Photography/Shutterstock, (B) Corey Rich/Aurora Photos/Alamy Stock Photo; **469** Klagyivik Viktor/Shutterstock; **471** (T) Felix Lipov/Shutterstock, (C) Skynesher/Vetta/Getty Images, (B) Stephen Vincent/Alamy Stock Photo; **472** (T) Sergiy Bykhunenko/Shutterstock, **472** (B) Gino Santa Maria/Shutterstock; **495** Nagel Photography/Shutterstock; **505** Ant Clausen/Fotolia; **507** (T) Peter Bernik/Shutterstock, (B) Westlee Jay Appleton/Shutterstock; **508** (T) Samuel Borges Photography/Shutterstock, (B) Steven Hogg/Shutterstock; **557** Yurakr/Shutterstock; **559** (T) EFesenko/Shutterstock, (C) Franck Boston/Shutterstock, (B) ESB Professional/Shutterstock; **560** SuriyaPhoto/Shutterstock; Studio Kiwi/Shutterstock, **568** StudioSmart/Shutterstock; **605** Bonita R. Cheshier/Shutterstock; **607** (T) Angelo Ferraris/Shutterstock, (B) Tanawat Palee/Shutterstock; **608** (B) Naramit/Shutterstock; (T) Business stock/Shutterstock, **628** Lledó/Fotolia; **637** (R) Ivonne Wierink/Fotolia, (L) Karichs/Fotolia; **639** (T) Karamysh/Shutterstock, (C) Noxnorthys/Shutterstock, (B) Gabriele Maltinti/Shutterstock; **640** Bowie15/123RF, Koya979/Shutterstock.